A TO Z OF HOUSING TERMINOLOGY

SIMON HOOTON

CHARTERED INSTITUTE OF HOUSING

The Chartered Institute of Housing

The Chartered Institute of Housing is the professional organisation for all people who work in housing. Its purpose is to take a strategic and leading role in encouraging and promoting the provision of good quality affordable housing for all. The Institute has more than 13,000 members working in local authorities, housing associations, the private sector and educational institutions.

Chartered Institute of Housing
Octavia House, Westwood Way
Coventry CV4 8JP
Telephone: 01203 694433

A to Z of Housing Terminology
Written by Simon Hooton

© Chartered Institute of Housing 1996

Published by the Chartered Institute of Housing

ISBN 1 900396 35 1

Design and layout by Jeremy Spencer
Cover illustration by Warwicks UK
Printed by Hobbs the Printers, Totton

INTRODUCTION

It is difficult to say whether housing has more jargon than other professions. It is much easier to say that there is an enormous amount of it and that a good argument probably exists for cutting down on its use. This book attempts to explain what the bewildering array of terms employed by housing officers actually means. Before understanding the issues which lie behind housing in Britain, one needs to first understand the language in which these problems are communicated. Perhaps, the language of housing has excluded too many people, for too long – if this book opens up housing to a wider range of people and makes it easier for all those involved to work together to improve the provision and management of housing, then it will have done its job.

The broad range of terminology used in housing highlights the wide range of issues upon which housing has an impact and the wide range of issues which affect the provision and management of housing in Britain today. This book has expanded continuously throughout its production to the point where there are nearly 1,400 entries on issues ranging from finance to welfare and housing law to special needs. I cannot pretend that this book contains all the terminology employed by the housing profession right across the country – many terms are only used locally and relate to very specific projects. I do hope that the vast majority of terms used nationally are contained within this book. If you feel that there are omissions then please contact the Chartered Institute of Housing and we will endeavour to incorporate your comments in future editions of the A to Z. The jargon contained within this book was, after all, generated by the profession and we ultimately rely on those working in and around housing to keep us up to date on the terms they use.

How to Use this Book

All terminology is listed alphabetically, with acronyms located at the beginning of their first letter group, eg **AMA** comes before **Abbeyfield Society**. All entries are cross-referenced – those terms which have their own definition are printed in bold. The definitions of terms listed as acronyms can be found under their full listing, eg:

CIS   **Cash Incentive Scheme**

A description of the Cash Incentive Scheme can be found under the full word entry, ie:

Cash Incentive Scheme   **DoE credit approvals** to **local authorities** to provide cash sums for **local authority tenants** to purchase homes on the open market, freeing up their present home for others in **housing need**.

The terms **DoE**, **credit approvals**, **local authority**, **tenants** and **housing need** each have entries of their own which can be found in the appropriate place.

ACKNOWLEDGEMENTS

The publication of this book was only possible with the invaluable assistance of a large number of people. In particular, I would like to thank:

Richard Bramley, Wakefield MDC
Ann Branson, Leicester City Council
Jane Brooke, Renfrewshire Council
John Bryant, NFHA
Vivian Chestnutt, Northern Ireland Housing Executive
Cllr Graham Facks-Martin, North Cornwall DC & National Housing Forum
Jane Gardner & John Acres, House Builders Federation
Michael Harmer, Tai Cymru
Cllr Peter Holt, LB Merton
Marianne Hood, TPAS
Cllr Tony Hooton, Vale Royal BC
Alan Kilburn, Home HA
John McHale, Knowlsey MBC
David Smith, Eastleigh Housing Association

Paul Brown, Legal Services Agency Ltd
Duncan Forbes, Solicitor.

And, many colleagues at the Chartered Institute of Housing including:
Louise Ayriss, Sarah Edwards, Alan Ferguson, Ross Fraser, Sam Lister, Alan McKeown, John Perry, Marian Reid, Janet Richards, Tamsin Sterling and Diane Wagstaff. And, those outside work who put up with my terminological condition, especially Ginny.

Many other sources have been used when compiling the definitions within this book, most notably the publications of a great many organisations contained within the library of the Chartered Institute of Housing – although too numerous to mention, I would like to acknowledge the input of the authors of these books.

ACAS	Advisory, Conciliation and Arbitration Service
ACC	Association of County Councils
ACE	Access Committee for England
ACE	Association for the Conservation of Energy
ACG	Acceptable Cost Guideline
ACG	Annual Capital Guideline
ACRE	Action with Communities in Rural England
ADC	Association of District Councils
ADLO	Association of Direct Labour Organisations
ADP	Approved Development Programme
ADSS	Association of Directors of Social Services
ADSW	Association of Directors of Social Work
AGM	annual general meeting
AHIT	Authorised Housing Investment Trust
AHP	approved HAG programme
AI	architect's instructions
ALA	Association of London Authorities
ALG	Association of London Government
ALS	approved landlord status
AMA	Association of Metropolitan Authorities
AMP	association monitoring profile
AONB	Area of Outstanding Natural Beauty
ARLA	Association of Residential Lettings Agents
abandoned property	A property in which no one is living and all the indications are that the occupants have left permanently and do not intend to return. In these circumstances there may have been an **implied surrender of tenancy**. After making enquiries about the **tenant's** whereabouts and posting a warning notice, **repossession** can take place without a **court order**.
abandonment notice	A notice served by a Scottish **landlord** on a **secure tenant** of an **abandoned property**: • stating the reasons for believing it is an **abandoned property** • requesting written notification from the **tenant** of their intention to reoccupy

- and, announcing that the **tenancy** will be terminated if after four weeks the **landlord** believes the **tenant** does not intend to reoccupy.

The notice needs to be delivered either in person or to the **tenant's** last known address.

abatement notice

Notice served by a **local authority** on a person responsible for a **statutory nuisance**, requiring them to stop the **nuisance** or remove the cause of the **nuisance** and where appropriate to prevent it from happening again. Failure to comply with the notice is a criminal offence and a person found guilty is liable to a fine up to level 5 on the standard scale (currently £5,000) and a further fine equal to one tenth of that amount for each day the nuisance continues. Failure to comply can also lead to the environmental health department seizing stereo equipment etc. Under Section 82 of the **Environmental Protection Act 1990** occupiers of premises that are a **statutory nuisance** or those affected by a **nuisance** can also bring proceedings in the magistrates court provided they have served the person responsible for the **nuisance** with a warning notice that they intend to do so.

Abbeyfield Society

Type of **housing association** which specialises in the small-scale provision of **supported housing** for the elderly, typically shared with a housekeeper.

abortive fees

Any payment which is made in respect of a scheme which is abandoned and does not come to fruition. Often used in the context of **development**.

absentee landlord

This term has no formal definition but is often used to describe a **landlord** who does not live in the rented property with the **tenant(s)**, who shows little or no interest in the property that they own and is often difficult for **tenants** to contact.

accelerated possession procedure

A court procedure which applies to **assured tenancies** in England & Wales and is intended to speed up the process of gaining **repossession** in cases where the **tenant** is unlikely to have a defence, eg where there is an **assured shorthold tenancy**. **Possession** proceedings can only be sped up in Scotland if the **tenant** improperly acquired the property by force or stealth.

Acceptable Cost Guideline

Indicative figure of the maximum **housing association development** costs by area, used by **Tai Cymru**.

accepted as homeless (England & Wales)

Statutory term for those who apply to a **local authority** for housing as a **homeless** household (or as being **threatened with homelessness**) and fulfil the statutory criteria set out in the **Housing Act 1996** of having:

1) no accommodation which they are entitled to occupy in the UK or elsewhere
2) accommodation, but –
   - cannot secure entry to it
   - it is a moveable structure, vehicle or vessel and they have nowhere to place it, where they are entitled to live in it
   - it is likely that occupation will lead to violence from another person living in it, or threats of violence from someone likely to carry out the threats

- it would be **unreasonable** for them to continue to occupy it
- it is not available for the whole household, ie the applicant and any other person who normally lives with them and with whom it is **reasonable** to expect them to live.

The **local authority** only has statutory duty to accept a household as homeless if they are:
- in **priority need**
- **unintentionally homeless**
- **eligible for assistance**
- and, there is no other suitable accommodation in the area.

At this stage, the authority will then consider whether the applicant has a **local connection** with any other authorities to which they may refer the applicant. If there is no **local connection** outside the area and all the other criteria are met, the authority must provide housing for the applicant.

accepted as homeless (Scotland)

Statutory term for those who apply to a **local authority** for housing as a **homeless** household (or as being **threatened with homelessness**) and fulfil the statutory criteria set out in the **Housing (Scotland) Act 1987** of having:
1) no accommodation which they are entitled to occupy
2) accommodation but –
   - cannot secure entry to it
   - it is a moveable structure, vehicle or vessel, unavailable for occupation
   - it is likely that occupation will lead to violence from some other person living in it or some other person who previously lived with the applicant whether in that accommodation or elsewhere
   - the accommodation is **statutorily overcrowded** and may endanger the health of the occupants
   - it would be **unreasonable** for them to continue to occupy it.

The **local authority** only has statutory duty to provide housing to households accepted as homeless if they are in **priority need**, **eligible for assistance, unintentionally homeless** and there is no other suitable accommodation in the area. At this stage, the authority may then consider whether the applicant has a **local connection** with any other authorities to which they may refer the applicant. If there is no **local connection** outside the area and all the other criteria are met, the authority must provide housing for the applicant.

Access Committee for England

Organisation which promotes the provision of accessible indoor and outdoor environments which enable disabled people to achieve their full potential and enter into public, social, intellectual, business and recreational life.

accountability

The notion that an individual or organisation is answerable to those with a stake in the policies and actions which it pursues, eg councillors of a **local authority** are accountable to the electorate, officers of the council are in turn accountable to councillors. Accountability in **housing associations** is less formal, officers are accountable to **board members** who are in turn accountable to the **members** of the association and the **national housing agency**.

accounting order

The **Statutory Instrument** which sets out the **statutory form of accounts** for **housing associations, SI 1992/512**.

Accounts Commission	See **Commission for Local Authority Accounts in Scotland**.
accruals accounting	Normal basis for commercial and national accounts. Revenue and expenditure are recorded when they accrue rather than when they are actually paid out and received as in a cash-based system.
accrued capital receipts	The total sum of **reserved receipts** held by a **local authority**.
acquisition allowance	Money paid by **Scottish Homes** to **housing associations** to cover the administration costs of acquiring new properties.
Acquisitions Initiative	See **Housing Market Package**.
Act of Parliament	Once a **Bill** has been passed by both Houses of Parliament (Commons & Lords) and received its **Royal Assent**, it becomes an Act of Parliament.
Action with Communities in Rural England	**ACRE** is the national association of **rural community councils** whose shared purpose is to improve quality of life of local communities and particularly of disadvantaged people in rural England.
actual rent	The rent which is charged on a dwelling as opposed to the **economic rent**.
adaptations	Physical changes made to a property to make it more suitable for a resident's needs, eg physically disabled residents.
adjudication officer	**Benefits Agency** employee responsible for determining an applicant's eligibility for welfare benefits and the levels of payment to which they are entitled.
adverse possession	Use or occupation of a plot of land or a building without permission from any other person for over 12 years which gives the occupier the right to claim ownership, eg **squatters**.
Advisory, Conciliation and Arbitration Service	Independent statutory body set up under the Employment Protection Act 1975 to provide conciliation and **mediation** and make facilities available for **arbitration** and issues codes of practice.
affordability ratio	A measure of the proportion of a household's income devoted to meeting housing costs. Used as an indicator for **affordable rents** along with the **residual income**.
affordable rents	A widely-used term, with no fixed definition, which prescribes a rent level considered to be appropriate given the income of **tenants**. Two measures are used to describe affordability, the **affordability ratio** and the **residual income** method.
Age Concern	Voluntary body which campaigns on behalf of older people and provides a wide range of services to meet their needs.
agency agreement	A **contract** between any organisations or individuals to deliver certain services.
Agenda 21	A programme of action for achieving **sustainable development** in the next century which came out of the Earth Summit in Rio 1992.

Local Agenda 21 refers to local programmes of action aimed at fulfilling the national requirements.

AIDS
Acquired Immune Deficiency Syndrome. People who are **HIV+**, have AIDS or AIDS-related conditions may require housing which makes it easier for them to access support networks, medical facilities and work, they may also need re-housing to avoid **harassment**. As the condition progresses, the resident may become wheelchair dependent and need other forms of support, which the house should be capable of accommodating.

allocations (England & Wales)
Process of letting properties to individuals. All **housing associations** and **local authorities** have **allocations policies** which set out the framework for deciding which households on their **housing register** receive which types of accommodation and in which order of priority. The **Housing Act 1996** requires **local authorities** to give **reasonable** preference to persons who:
- occupy insanitary or **overcrowded** houses
- live in unsatisfactory conditions
- live in temporary accommodation or occupy their homes on insecure terms
- have dependent children (or are expecting children)
- have a medical or welfare need for settled accommodation
- are in social or economic circumstances which mean they have difficulty in securing settled accommodation.

Central government can make regulations setting out the principles for **allocation policies** and also set out factors which **local authorities** cannot take into account in their **allocation policies**. **Registered social landlords** must subscribe to the **Tenants' Guarantee** which restricts them to providing accommodation for those in **housing need** for whom suitable housing is not available at prices within their means. **Local authorities** and **registered social landlords** must publish a summary of their **allocation policies** and provide these free of charge on request.

allocations (Scotland)
Scottish authorities' **waiting lists** are constrained by Section 19(1)a of the **Housing (Scotland) Act 1987** which prevents the authority from taking account of the applicant's:
- length of residence in the area
- outstanding **liability** for rent, if accrued when they were not the **tenant**
- age (providing they are over 16)
- income
- past **tenure**, particularly if they are former **owner-occupiers**

and they cannot impose conditions on eligibility for re-housing by requiring that:
- the application must be in force for a certain period of time
- a divorce or judicial separation be obtained
- the applicant be living alone.

allocations policy
Statement of a **landlord's** criteria for allocating housing. This will usually be differentiated by client group, property size, area etc and may deal with specific issues relating to **supported housing**, eg a **housing association** specialising in homes for the elderly will give a low priority to (or even exclude) applicants under a certain age.

allowable costs	Costs which in the **CCT** process may be deducted from the **in-house team's** bid before **tenders** are compared and evaluated.
almshouse trust	Type of charitable housing dating back to the twelfth century. It was traditionally financed by Christian benefactors to provide housing for the poor and those who had fallen on hard times. The almshouse movement is headed by the **National Association of Almshouses** which is part of the voluntary housing movement and receives funding from the **national housing agency**.
Annual Capital Guideline	The total **capital expenditure** allocated to a **local authority** by **central government**. The **ACG** for housing is based, in part, on each authority's **GNI** (40%) whilst the remainder is determined at the discretion of the **Secretary of State**. From 1997/8 onwards, allocation of **ACG** will be entirely competitive at the **local authority** level, but **GNI** will still be used to determine regional allocations.
annual general meeting	Meeting of all shareholders and/or members of an organisation. Nearly all **housing associations** must hold an **AGM** at which **board members** are elected and audited accounts and the annual report are presented.
annual lettings plan	See **annual re-housing plan**.
annual re-housing plan	A plan drawn up by a **local authority**, in consultation with other **social housing** providers and referral agencies which sets out targets and monitoring procedures for re-housing the various need groups in the locality over the coming year. Also known as **annual lettings plan**.
annuity mortgage	Conventional form of **mortgage** arrangement whereby the borrower makes monthly payments to repay the **principal** and cover any interest which has accrued on a debt to the lender (secured on the property itself).
anti-competitive behaviour	Actions which restrict, prevent or distort the competitive process. The **CCT** process should be free from anti-competitive behaviour.
anti-social behaviour	Behaviour that falls below society's norms and accepted standards of behaviour. This can include criminal acts and less serious **nuisance** such as dumping rubbish. The term has no legal status and is open to many interpretations.
appeal	A term which is used in many contexts to describe the process of querying an adjudication. An appeal against the decision of an **adjudication officer** relating to **social security benefits** is heard by an independent tribunal. Applicants who are refused planning permission by their **local authority** can appeal to the **Secretary of State**. The final course of appeal for many is through the law courts.
Applicable Amount	The total assumed requirements of a claimant for a **means tested** benefit, ie it is an assessment of the applicants assumed needs. It is made up from the **Personal Allowance** and any **Premium(s)**. This is then compared with the claimant's actual income to determine the amount paid.

Appropriate Rent	The **reasonable** market rent for a property on which a **Housing Benefit** claim is being made. The Appropriate Rent is the lowest of either the **Property Specific Rent** or the **Size Related Rent**. The maximum **Housing Benefit** is then calculated by comparing the Appropriate Rent with the **Local Reference Rent**.
approved agencies	Organisations in England & Wales given formal approval by the **DoE** to undertake work to assist **tenants'** participation and **right to manage** with **Section 16 grants**.
Approved Development Programme	The **national housing agencies'** annual cash limit for **capital expenditure** on **housing association** projects. The ADP is distributed among **housing associations** through the allocation of **HAG** for approved developments.
approved development status	Conferred on Welsh **housing associations** by **Tai Cymru** allowing them to carry out their own development programme.
approved HAG programme status	Conferred on a **local authority** by the **Housing Corporation**, giving it authorisation to fund **housing association** projects through **LAHAG** without first seeking approval from the **Housing Corporation**. Very few **local authorities** have **AHP** status as they need to have a track record of supporting **LAHAG** programmes and be funding 20 projects in the first year of approval.
approved landlord scheme	**Local authority** scheme for accrediting **private rented sector landlords** whose properties meet certain pre-defined environmental health standards. There is no statutory obligation upon **local authorities** to run such a scheme and consequently the eligibility criteria vary from scheme to scheme. They are often tied in with a **rent guarantee** for participating **landlords**.
approved landlord status	Accreditation from the **national housing agency** required by all **landlords** which wish to take over the ownership and management of **housing stock** under the **Tenants' Choice** scheme. The term continues to apply in Scotland and to organisations wishing to take over **housing stock** from a **Housing Action Trust**.
arbitration	Procedure for settling disputes between two parties, eg a **contractor** and a **client**. Both parties agree to the binding conclusion of the independent arbitrator before the process begins. The **Chartered Institute of Housing** offers an arbitration service in conjunction with the Chartered Institute of Arbitrators for settling contractual disputes in the field of housing.
architect's brief	Instructions given by a **client** to an architect outlining the work which is required.
architect's certificates	Document giving the architect's approval to a **contractor's** bill. Receipt of such a certificate is required before the **client** will pay for the **contractor's** work.
architect's instructions	Instruction issued by an architect in writing, usually to notify the **client** of a change in the **contract**.

area board	Municipal body in Northern Ireland responsible for delivering public services. Each board consists of a mix of **district council** members and ministerial appointees. There are four Health and Personal Social Services Boards and five Education & Public Libraries Boards.
Area of Outstanding Natural Beauty	Area designated by a **local authority** and **central government** where development is restricted.
asset	A physical or monetary item of value, eg land, property, shares etc.
asset creation	The generation of value or earning power. The building or acquisition of new properties by a **landlord** can be described as **asset creation**.
assignation	See **assignment**.
assignment	Transfer of a **tenancy** from the **tenant** to another person. This should be done by a **deed** or a **court order**. For **secure tenancies** and **assured tenancies**, assignments can take place during a **mutual exchange**. Otherwise, assignments of **secure tenancies** can only take place:
	• where there has been a divorce and the court has ordered an assignment
	• to a person who has the right to the **tenancy** by **succession**.
	Registered housing associations are required by the **Tenants' Guarantee** to allow assignment of an **assured tenancy** following an order of the court in divorce or by way of exchange but are not obliged to allow assignment to persons who qualify for the **tenancy** by **succession**. Known as **assignation** in Scotland.
Association for the Conservation of Energy	Organisation which promotes awareness of the benefits of energy conservation and lobbies for policy change. Membership is made up of private companies in the energy conservation industry.
association monitoring profile	Brief description of a **housing association's** activities drawn up by **Scottish Homes** and used when devising **cash planning targets**.
Association of County Councils	Representative body of **county councils** in England & Wales. Its objectives are to promote and protect the interests of member councils and of **local government** in general and to disseminate information. The **ACC** is set to merge with the **ADC** and **AMA** to form the **Local Government Association** in 1997. Until the creation of the **LGA**, the **ACC** and **ADC** will jointly represent the vast majority of the new **unitary authorities** in England & Wales.
Association of Direct Labour Organisations	Representative body of direct service provision (including **direct labour organisations**). The **ADLO** provides its members with information on the latest developments in **CCT** and related issues, offers advice and research facilities, lobbies government and provides a regular journal and briefing papers.
Association of Directors of Social Services	The professional body of directors of social services in England, Wales & Northern Ireland. The **ADSS** comments on and advises on all issues within the social services field and publishes a quarterly bulletin. Its Scottish counterpart is the **ADSW**.
Association of Directors of Social Work	Professional body of social workers and social services officers in Scotland.

Association of District Councils	Representative body of **district councils** in England & Wales. Its objectives are to protect and further the interests of **district councils** and to promote the interests of **local government** in general. The **ADC** is set to merge with the **ACC** and **AMA** to form the **Local Government Association** in 1997. Until the creation of the **LGA**, the ADC and **ACC** will jointly represent the vast majority of the new **unitary authorities** in England & Wales.
Association of London Authorities	Consultation forum for London authorities to present their views to **central government**. The **ALA** has now merged with the **London Boroughs Association** to form the **Association of London Government**.
Association of London Government	Unified body representing the views of **local authorities** in London. Formed out of the **ALA** and **LBA.**
Association of Metropolitan Authorities	**Local government** body representing the views of **metropolitan authorities** (including the London boroughs) in England. The **AMA's** objectives are to watch over, protect and promote the interests, rights, powers and duties of its member authorities and to provide a forum for discussion of matters of common concern to its members. The **AMA** is set to merge with the **ACC** and **ADC** to form the **Local Government Association** in 1997.
Association of Residential Lettings Agents	Membership body representing the views of **landlords** in the **private rented sector**. It disseminates information on legislative changes to its membership, promotes good practice and acts as an accreditation body for residential lettings agents through a professional indemnity insurance scheme.
assured shorthold tenancy	Time limited **assured tenancy** used in the **private rented sector** (and occasionally by **housing associations**). It is possible to use an **accelerated possession procedure** in England & Wales to regain **possession** when the period of the **tenancy** has expired. This procedure enables the court to make an **order for possession** without having a hearing. The minimum length of an assured shorthold tenancy is 6 months, but they often last for 12 months. Under the **Housing Act 1996** in England & Wales, unless a **tenant** is explicitly informed otherwise, their **tenancy** is an assured shorthold. Known as **short assured tenancies** in Scotland.
assured tenancy	Type of **tenancy** created by the **Housing Act 1988**. The **tenant** must occupy the dwelling as her/his only or principal home. An assured tenancy gives **security of tenure** to the **tenant**. The **landlord** can only gain **possession** of the dwelling with a **court order** and must prove to the court that **grounds for possession** apply, eg **rent arrears**, **nuisance**, breach of tenancy, etc. An assured tenancy may be a **fixed term tenancy** or a **periodic tenancy**. Most **tenancies** granted by **housing associations** since 1989 have been assured tenancies. One kind of assured tenancy is an **assured shorthold tenancy** and these are the most commonly used in the **private rented sector**.
asylum-seeker	A person claiming asylum in the UK. The eligibility of asylum-seekers for housing assistance is currently subject to change.

attachment of earnings
Legal method for recovering a debt by which a creditor can request deductions from the wages of a debtor direct from the debtor's employer. The creditor must have obtained a **judgment** for the debt from the court before being able to use attachment of earnings. For example **landlords** can use attachment of earnings to recover **rent arrears** from **tenants**. Known as **earnings arrestment** in Scotland.

Attendance Allowance
A **non-means tested, non-contributory, social security benefit** to cover the cost of personal care or supervision for disabled people over the age of 65. This term is also used in conjunction with councillors expenses for attending council meetings.

audit
Investigation of an organisation's objectives, measurable standards of performance, organisational structures and/or financial accounts.

Audit Commission
A statutory body which appoints **district auditors** to **local authorities** and the NHS in England & Wales. The Commission carries out national studies of value for money, aims to promote proper stewardship of public finances and assist those responsible for public services to achieve economy, efficiency and effectiveness.

audit trail
An assessment of the systems employed in an organisation, with particular emphasis on the chain of responsibility for income and expenditure, used to establish financial effectiveness. Audit trails are also used in the assessment of repairs, **void** management and **homeless** systems.

Authorised Housing Investment Trust
See **Housing Investment Trust**.

B&B	**Bed & Breakfast**
BCA	**Basic Credit Approval**
BES	**Business Expansion Scheme**
BRE	**Building Research Establishment**
BRECSU	**Building Research Energy Conservation Unit**
BREEAM	**Building Research Establishment Environmental Assessment Method**
BS	British Standard
BSA	**Building Societies Association**
BTS	**Below the Tolerable Standard**
Back-To-Work Bonus	A one off £1,000 payment to the long-term unemployed when they start work under the **Job Seeker's Allowance**.
bad debts	Debts which it is assumed will never be recovered and are written off, eg after a period of time **former tenants' arrears** become **write offs**.
bailiff	There are two kinds of bailiff:

1) a county court bailiff is a civil servant employed by the court whose job it is to enforce **court orders**. Only a county court bailiff can **evict** a **tenant** under a county court **possession order**. Bailiffs can also enforce court **judgments** for debts by seizing and selling the debtor's goods.
2) a certificated bailiff is a private **contractor** who has been granted a certificate by the local county court judge. Certificated bailiffs authorised by **landlords** can in some cases collect **rent arrears** by seizing any goods in the dwelling and selling them to pay the debt. **Landlords** in the **private rented sector** need the court's permission to use bailiffs in this way but **housing associations** and **local authorities** do not.
In Scotland, they are known as **sheriff officers** or **messengers at arms**.

bank overdraft guarantee	A facility to allow **Scottish Homes** to underwrite the overdrafts of **housing associations**.
barrier free	Design concept employed in housing intended for people with disabilities. A barrier free home should allow full wheelchair and pushchair access and mobility.
Basic Credit Approval	Amount of money **central government** allows each **local authority** to borrow for **capital expenditure** as part of its **Housing Investment Programme**.
Bed & Breakfast	Short-stay accommodation traditionally associated with holidays, but of late many **local authorities** have used **B&B** to temporarily house households **accepted as homeless**.

Below the Tolerable Standard	Statutory definition of inadequate housing, only used in Scotland. A property only meets the standard if it: • is structurally stable • is substantially free from rising or penetrating damp • has satisfactory provision for lighting, ventilation and heating • has adequate water supply • has a sink providing hot and cold water • provides exclusive use of an inside toilet • has an effective system for the drainage and disposal of water • has satisfactory facilities for cooking within the house • has satisfactory access to all external doors and outbuildings. In the rest of the UK **Unfit for Human Habitation** is used as the statutory standard.
Benefits Agency	An agency of the **Department of Social Security**, with responsibility for administering **social security benefits**. NB this excludes **Housing Benefit** and **Council Tax** Benefit which are administered by the **local authority**.
Bill	Proposed legislation debated by Parliament on its way to becoming an **Act of Parliament**.
bill of quantity	Statement in the contracting process outlining the work commissioned and the procedure for assessment.
Black & Minority Ethnic Housing Association Strategy	**Housing Corporation** strategy to promote black and minority ethnic **housing associations**.
black housing association	A **housing association** which has 80% Black, Asian, Caribbean or South East Asian representation on its **board of management** and aims to meet ethnic minority **housing needs**.
blemished title	Land which has **restrictive covenants** attached to it which limit the uses to which the land can be put in the future, eg it must always be used for the provision of housing at **affordable rents**. The value of the land is reduced by such **restrictive covenants**.
block A properties	Pre-1988 **housing association** houses which are not eligible for **HAG** funding to cover the cost of **major repairs**.
block B properties	Pre-1988 **housing association** houses which remain eligible for **HAG** funding to cover the cost of **major repairs**.
block repairs	See **enveloping**.
board member	Member of the **board of management** of a **housing association, Housing Investment Trust, Housing Action Trust, local housing company** etc.
board of management	Governing body of a **housing association** (or any other organisation) elected from its membership. The committee usually has between 7 and 15 members. In most **housing associations**, each year, one third of **board members** must stand for re-election. Typically, up to 5 co-opted members are permitted but are not eligible to vote on matters concerning membership or officers of the association. Usually, the committee must meet at least 3 times a year and quorum is achieved

when 3 are in attendance (excluding co-opted members). Committee members are responsible for policy making, control, custody of funds and act as employer, **landlord** and ambassador.

bond	A financial investment product issued by governments, companies, banks etc which bears interest (usually fixed) and often with a **redemption** date at which time the investment is refunded.
borough council	Elected municipal body with a charter to have a mayor. It may be a **metropolitan authority** or a **district council**.
borough valuer	**Local government** official with responsibility for the valuation of land or property in which the **local authority** has an interest.
boundary commission	See **Local Government Commission for England, Local Government Boundary Commission for Scotland, Local Government Boundary Commission for Wales** or **Boundary Commission for Northern Ireland**.
Boundary Commission for Northern Ireland	Government body with responsibility for reviewing **local government** ward boundaries. **Local government** in Northern Ireland has retained the same structure since 1973, with 26 **district councils** and 9 **area boards**.
break clause	Clause in any form of **contract** which allows for one party to escape the requirements of the **contract**, eg in **Housing Management CCT contracts, tenants** can exercise their **right to manage** through a break clause.
bridging interest	Interest charged on loans taken out to cover expenditure incurred during the **development** of a housing project, also known as **capitalised interest**. The interest is added to the **principal** sum borrowed.
brown field site	A development location which has previously been built on or used, as opposed to a **green field site**.
Brundtland Report	A report for the World Commission on Environment & Development actually titled *Our Common Future*. Noted for its definition and promotion of **sustainable development**.
BS 5750	The British Standard which lays down the accepted standard for quality systems in management. Many **housing associations** and **local authorities** pursue management policies based on BS 5750.
BS 7750	British Standards' **eco-auditing** scheme. Broadly similar to **EMAS** but designed for all types of organisation and does not require the publication of audit results.
buddy partner	1) Someone who provides informal assistance and comfort to a person with a particular social or medical need, eg people with **AIDS**.
	2) A relationship between a large and a small **housing association** whereby the smaller organisation utilises the resources of the larger one, eg access to its computer facilities and **housing register**.

Budgeting Loan

An interest free, discretionary loan from the **Social Fund** to help with one off expenses incurred by long-term **Income Support** claimants.

building regulation approval

Approval for the construction of a building in accordance with **building regulations**.

building regulations

Legal minimum standards and procedures which construction projects must keep to.

Building Research Energy Conservation Unit

Division of the **BRE** with responsibility for **energy efficiency**.

Building Research Establishment

Executive agency of the **Department of the Environment** which provides advice and carries out research into the design and performance of buildings, their constituent materials and the prevention and control of fire, in order to improve the performance of built works and the construction industry.

Building Research Establishment Environmental Assessment Method

Standard **environmental audit** for homes, offices and supermarkets developed by the **BRE.** It focuses very closely on the ecological impact of individual buildings rather than the wider environmental considerations included in **EMAS.**

Building Societies Association

Representative body of **building societies**. It provides a range of services and lobbies government on behalf of its membership. Closely associated with the **CML.**

building society

Lending and savings organisation owned by its **members** and originally set up to provide finance for housing. Today banks compete very directly against building societies in the **mortgage** market, although many building societies are now converting to banks.

building warrant

Document which must be obtained from the **local authority's** building control department in Scotland to approve the structure of proposed works.

Business Expansion Scheme

Government scheme providing tax relief to investors in residential property. It was aimed at boosting the **private rented sector** by exempting shareholders in **BES** companies from Income Tax and **CGT**. It is currently being phased out.

business plan

A statement of an organisation's plans and goals for the future, usually in financial terms. Often used to convince potential funders of the viability of a particular project or the organisation itself.

CAB	**Citizens' Advice Bureau**
CAT	**Credit Approval Transfer**
CBHA	**Community Based Housing Association**
CCT	**Compulsory Competitive Tendering**
CCTV	closed circuit television
CGT	**Capital Gains Tax**
CHAR	Campaign for the Homeless And Roofless. A national membership organisation which works through its members to help **homeless** and badly housed single people gain access to decent, affordable accommodation and the means to sustain it.
CHAS	**Catholic Housing Aid Service**
CHICL	**Community Homes In Central London**
CHP	**Combined Heat & Power**
CIEH	**Chartered Institute of Environmental Health**
CIH	**Chartered Institute of Housing**
CIPFA	**Chartered Institute of Public Finance & Accountancy**
CIS	**Cash Incentive Scheme**
CML	**Council of Mortgage Lenders**
CORE	**Continuous Recording of New Lettings**
COSLA	**Convention of Scottish Local Authorities**
CPAG	**Child Poverty Action Group**
CPO	compulsory purchase order
CPRE	**Council for the Protection of Rural England**
CRE	**Commission for Racial Equality**
CSA	**Child Support Agency**
CTI	**Comprehensive Tenement Improvement**
Cabinet Office	**Central government** department responsible for many cross-departmental issues such as the **Citizen's Charter**, public appointments, the civil service and efficiency in government management.
CADW	Welsh Historic Monuments, the **quango** responsible for the conservation, marketing and management of historic monuments in Wales.

Campaign for Bedsit Rights	Campaign group working to improve the bad conditions and poor standards of management in **HMOs** in England & Wales. Its membership is drawn from **housing advice services, local authorities, tenants' associations**, student unions and law centres. It attempts to achieve its goals through media work, lobbying ministers and producing publications.
capital allocation	The total **capital expenditure** available to **local authorities** in Scotland. This is made up of **permissions to borrow** and **capital receipts**.
Capital Challenge	A **DoE** scheme to encourage **local authorities** to bid competitively for **Supplementary Credit Approvals** to finance their **capital expenditure** programmes. The pilot Capital Challenge scheme will commence in 1997/8. **Local authorities** have been invited to submit bids in respect of any **capital expenditure** plans they may have.
capital expenditure	Money spent on projects which creates, purchases or increases the value of a fixed **asset**, ie which delivers a lasting benefit over a period of years, as opposed to **revenue expenditure**.
Capital Gains Tax	Tax levied on increases in the value of capital **assets**, eg shares. It is levied at the same rate as the basic rate of Income Tax.
capital receipts	Money received from the sale of capital **assets**. The main source of capital receipts for **local authorities** is from the sale of council housing and land. In England & Wales, **local authorities** can only invest **usable receipts** in new projects, the remainder must be kept as **reserved** or **set-aside receipts**. **Local authorities** in Scotland must use 25% of their capital receipts to pay off debts and can use the remainder as they choose.
capital sum	See **principal**.
capital value	Value of a property used to calculate **capital value rents**.
capital value rent	A rent based (at least in part) on the current **capital value** of the dwelling.
capitalised interest	The interest on a scheme represented as a lump sum added to the outstanding debt at today's value.
capitalised repairs	Repairs to the **housing stock** which contribute to the **capital value** of the dwellings. They are financed out of the **landlord's capital expenditure** programme rather than **revenue expenditure**.
care & repair	Like **staying-put**, care & repair schemes assist older **owner-occupiers** and those with physical disabilities, wishing to stay in their current homes as their support needs grow. However, care & repair only aims to assist people to carry out major works which require **house renovation grants**.
care contracts	A **contract** between two parties for one to provide care services on the other's behalf, eg a **housing association** may undertake care duties under a **contract** with the local social services department.
Care in the Community	Government policy to shift provision of housing and related services for people with special needs from hospitals and other institutions to community-based facilities. The concept of **community care** predated

Care in the Community but was restructured and formalised by the **NHS and Community Care Act 1990.**

Cash Incentive Scheme

DoE credit approvals to **local authorities** to provide cash sums for **local authority tenants** to purchase homes on the open market, freeing up their present home for others in **housing need.**

cash limited allocation

Annual sum of money allocated to Welsh **housing associations** by **Tai Cymru.**

cash limits

Treasury restrictions on the amount of public money spent, or authorised to be spent, by each government department.

cash planning target

A mechanism for ensuring that the sum of separate expenditures does not exceed aggregate limits, eg **HAG** funding for individual **housing associations** in an area should not exceed the limit set out in the **Housing Corporation's regional allocation statement.**

cash programme

Statement of agreement between the **national housing agency** and a **housing association** that a given number of properties of a defined type and in a specified location will be provided in return for an agreed **HAG** payment.

cash-flow forecast

Prediction of future in- and out-flows of money from an organisation.

catch-up repairs

Property repairs which bring a dwelling up to the standard which could **reasonably** be expected if it had been well maintained. Catch-up repairs specifically exclude improvements to the dwelling. This is a concept used in **LSVT** to assess the repairs burden the new owner will inherit.

Category 1 Housing

Self-contained **sheltered housing** designed for older residents, defined in government Circular 82/69.

Category 2 Housing

Grouped flats aimed at meeting the housing and support needs of less active older people, generally with **warden** coverage, defined in government Circular 82/69.

Category 2.5 Housing

An unofficial term for housing for frail elderly people whose needs exceed the service provided by **warden** coverage but who do not require continuous care, eg meal delivery and home-help services may be available, but waking night cover is not.

Catholic Housing Aid Service

A voluntary organisation that offers free and confidential housing advice and support through its 10 advice centres to anyone in **housing need.** It has an education programme which aims to encourage groups and individuals to campaign for the rights of **homeless** people.

CECODHAS

European liaison committee for **social housing.** It is an **NGO** which aims to represent the views of its member federations and European **social housing** beneficiaries. It works to facilitate co-operation between members and to increase the economic, technical and social efficiency of members organisations and to promote **social housing** for all Europeans. UK members include **NFHA, NIFHA, NIHE, SFHA** and **WFHA.**

central government	National government. Throughout this book central government is used to refer to United Kingdom government as opposed to **local government**.
certificate of practical completion	Notification from the architect to the **client** stating that construction work is complete.
challenge fund	Pool of money available to applicants on a competitive basis. Examples include resources for the **Single Regeneration Budget** and the **Estates Renewal Challenge Fund**.
Chancellor of The Duchy of Lancaster	Cabinet level minister responsible for the **Office of Public Service & Science (OPSS)** and the **Citizen's Charter**.
charitable housing association	**Housing association** with charitable status. These bodies may by **registered charities** or **exempt charities**. Charity status confers tax advantages on the association, but restricts the scope of its **objects**. Typically a charitable **housing association** is restricted to providing housing and associated amenities to people on low income or people with special needs, eg people with disabilities or the elderly.
Charity Commission	Government body responsible for registration of charities in England & Wales. It has powers to investigate and remedy mal-administration and abuse. The vast majority of **charitable housing associations** are not registered with the Charity Commission, but instead with the **Registrar of Friendly Societies**. In Scotland, regulation of charities is carried out within the **Scottish Office**.
charity trustees	The individuals who are responsible for the management of a charity. They may be described as trustees, directors, **board members** or committee members.
Charter Mark	Award within the **Citizen's Charter** initiative for excellence in delivering a public service. The awards are administered by the **Office of Public Service & Science (OPSS)** but final decisions are made by the Prime Minister's **Citizen's Charter** Advisory Panel and the **Chancellor of The Duchy of Lancaster**. All Charter Mark winners can use the Charter Mark logo for three years on their promotional material. Nine criteria are used: • standards • information and openness • choice and consultation • courtesy and helpfulness • putting things right • value for money • customer satisfaction • measurable improvement in quality of service • innovative enhancements to service without extra cost to consumer or tax payer.
Chartered Institute of Environmental Health	The professional and educational body of environmental health officers, formerly known as the **Institution of Environmental Health Officers**.
Chartered Institute of Housing	Professional body representing all those working in housing, it promotes the provision and management of good quality, affordable housing for all. **CIH** administers qualifications for housing staff,

provides training courses, promotes good practice and represents the views of the housing profession to government and the general public.

Chartered Institute of Public Finance & Accountancy
Professional accounting body for the public sector, including **central** and **local government**, the health service, the water industry and other **public corporations**. It publishes statistics on **local authority Housing Revenue Accounts**, **capital expenditure**, debt, rents and **homelessness**.

chief rent
See **ground rent**.

Child Benefit
A **non-means tested**, **non-contributory**, **social security benefit** paid to the parents (or guardian) of children under the age of 16 (extended to 19 for those in education). Previously called **Family Allowance**.

Child Poverty Action Group
Voluntary organisation campaigning to alleviate family poverty in the UK with a particular focus on social security issues. Also publishes advice handbooks on welfare benefits including **Housing Benefit** and **Council Tax** Benefit.

Child Support Agency
Government agency with responsibility for assessing the maintenance payable by absent parents to child carers.

Citizen's Charter
A **central government** scheme to promote quality in public services. **Local authorities** are under a statutory duty to produce **performance indicators** for local people (including **tenants**) which are published nationally by the **Audit Commission**. Organisations with responsibility for delivering public services can also be considered for a **Charter Mark**.

Citizens' Advice Bureau
Independent advice service providing free, confidential and impartial advice on a wide range of social security, debt, housing, employment, legal, tax, immigration and discrimination issues. **NACAB** is the national umbrella organisation for local **CAB**x.

Citizens' Advice Scotland
Scottish equivalent of **NACAB**.

City Challenge
DoE scheme providing funds for **capital expenditure** to partnership schemes aiming to regenerate local communities. The partnerships usually include **local authorities**, private sector bodies and voluntary organisations. City Challenge has now been superseded by the **Single Regeneration Budget**.

City of London Corporation
Unique form of **local authority** responsible for the City of London (the Square Mile). Consists of the Lord Mayor, 24 aldermen and 132 common councilmen. It manages a stock of 3,000 council homes situated across London plus 2,000 flats in the Barbican.

City Summit
See **Habitat II**.

clearance area
An area of properties which has been designated for demolition by a **local authority**. Under the Housing Act 1957, clearance areas must contain homes which are **Unfit for Human Habitation** (or injurious

to the health of the inhabitants) and it must be shown that the most satisfactory method of dealing with the conditions is the demolition of all buildings in the area. Today, **Renewal Areas** have largely replaced clearance areas.

client

Organisation or individual which receives a service under a **contract**. In **CCT**, the client specifies the service that it requires under the **contract** and lets the **contract** after deciding between competing **contractors**.

client-agent

An organisation or individual used by a **client** to manage a **contract** on their behalf, eg a firm of consultants or architects.

client-contractor split

The division of an organisation into the two parties of a **contract**; the **client** and the **contractor**. Usually associated with an **in-house team's** tender for a **CCT contract**. The **contractor** will usually have to compete for the **contract** with other external bodies, eg private sector organisations in a **tendering** process. The split defines which responsibilities fall to each party of the **contract**.

closing order

A **local authority** order placed on a property prohibiting its use for any purpose not approved by the **local authority**. The order usually prohibits the use of the property as a dwelling. Where a building contains flats, a closing order can be made in relation to individual flats.

cluster flats

Collection of homes which share certain services, eg kitchens and bathrooms. Usually associated with **supported housing** projects.

Code of Governance

An **NFHA** document which recommends best practice in the governance of **housing associations**. The code covers the role and constitution of the **board of management**, the responsibilities of the chair, the duties of the chief executive, openness, **tenant participation**, **equal opportunities policies**, management **audit** and the core values of **NFHA** members.

Code of Practice for Rented Housing

Code published by the **Commission for Racial Equality** on the operation of the Race Relations Act 1976 in relation to all rented housing and the elimination of associated racial discrimination. Although the Code does not impose any legal obligations, its provisions are admissible as evidence in legal proceedings under the Race Relations Act.

cold bridging

Phenomenon whereby cold is conducted by a physical element of the building from its outside to the inside. Most common in concrete **system built** tower blocks. All modern buildings have a cavity between the inner and outer skins to avoid cold bridging.

Combined Heat & Power

Method of energy production often used in tower blocks or on estates. A dedicated turbine generates both heating and electricity. Heat released by electricity generating turbines is harnessed to provide warmth. The system can produce fuel to power ratios of up to 80% compared with 35% in traditional coal fired power stations.

Combined Heat & Power Association

Organisation which promotes the use of **Combined Heat & Power** systems.

Commission for Local Authority Accounts in Scotland	Government body with responsibility for auditing the accounts of **local authorities** and advising on accounting matters in Scotland. Also known as the **Accounts Commission.** Its counterpart in England & Wales is the **Audit Commission**.
Commission for Racial Equality	Statutory body working towards the elimination of discrimination and promoting equality of opportunity and good relations between ethnic groups.
committee of management	See **board of management**.
Committee Stage	Following the **Second Reading** of a **Bill's** passage through the House of Commons, a **Standing Committee** of MPs (or peers) examines the **Bill** clause by clause and amendments are considered and voted on. The composition of the Committee reflects the balance of the parties in the Commons.
common allocation policy	An agreed and unified **allocations policy** among housing providers in a locality where a **common housing register** is in operation. All **landlords** participating in the policy apply the same needs assessment and selection criteria for offering tenancies.
common housing register	An arrangement between a **local authority** and **registered social landlords** (and possibly private **landlords**) in the area to collectively receive applications for housing and to register **housing need** using a common administrative procedure. **Landlords** are then free to offer **tenancies** to households on the register according to their own **allocations policy**. Unlike **common allocations policies**, common housing registers do not dictate **allocations** criteria to **landlords**.
Community Based Housing Association	A **housing association** set up to acquire and **rehabilitate** dwellings. Such associations are community run, have strong connections to the locality in which they operate and often have **tenant** majorities on the **board of management**.
community care	Concept that care services should be delivered to people in their homes (including residential nursing homes) wherever possible. It is underpinned by a belief that people with special care needs will lead more fulfilling and independent lives if they live in the community rather than institutions. Formalised in the government initiative **Care in the Community**.
Community Care Grant	A **Social Fund** payment to enable an individual to move out of, or avoid going into institutional care.
Community Care Implementation Unit	Organisation which monitors and assists in the implementation of **community care** legislation and the development of policy in Scotland. The unit comprises representatives of the NHS Management Executive, **Social Work Services Group** and the **Scottish Office Development Department**.
Community Charge	System of **local government** taxation which replaced **Rates** in April 1990 but was withdrawn in March 1993. It was a **regressive** tax under which each adult over 18 was charged a flat rate. Also known as the **Poll Tax**. It was replaced by the **Council Tax**.

community council	See **local council**.
Community Development Foundation	Voluntary sector body which seeks to ensure the effective participation of people in determining the conditions which affect their lives by providing support, promoting best practice and informing policy makers.
Community Homes In Central London	A federation of community groups from central London which aims to provide a voice for community life in the centre of the Capital, monitor the impact of housing and planning policies on communities in the Capital and develop innovative policies to support neighbourhood life.
community ownership	Informal term to describe an estate which has been **transferred** from **local authority** ownership to a **community-based housing association**.
company limited by guarantee	An organisation registered under the Companies Act 1985 with the Registrar of Companies in England & Wales. **Members** of the company guarantee to pay a fixed sum (usually £1) if the organisation becomes insolvent. Membership is personal and not transferable, ie membership rights cannot be sold. **Members** are usually responsible for electing the company's **board of management**, though places on the board may be reserved for individuals nominated by other organisations, eg a **local authority**. Some **housing associations** are companies limited by guarantee whilst also being **registered charities**. The directors of companies limited by guarantee are almost always unpaid.
company limited by shares	An organisation registered under the Companies Act 1985 with the Registrar of Companies in England & Wales. The company is owned by the shareholders but in the event of the company becoming insolvent, the shareholders **liability** is limited to the amount of their shareholding. Company debts cannot be recovered from shareholders' private **assets**. Unlike **companies limited by guarantee**, companies limited by shares trade for profit. They may be public (Plc), ie they have their shares listed on the Stock Exchange, or private (Ltd) where shares are not publicly traded but can generally be transferred. The rules of the company sometimes limit the persons who can become shareholders. The directors of companies limited by shares are generally paid.
compensation for improvements	See **right to compensation for improvements**.
competition requirement	Amount of **defined activity** which an authority must put out to **tender** under **CCT**.
competitive HIP	As from 1997/8, in England **HIP** funds will be allocated to each **local authority** on a competitive basis. Previously a portion has been decided using **GNI**. The regional allocation will continue to be allocated using the **GNI**.
competitive tendering	Process of inviting offers from outside organisations to run a specified service. The **tender** process is competitive and decisions are usually made against a set of pre-determined criteria which incorporate quality and scope of service as well as price.

completions	Number of dwellings built over a period of time.
Comprehensive Tenement Improvement	Scheme within **Scottish Homes' ADP** for improving areas with high densities of **tenement** flats.
Comptroller and Auditor General	Director of the **National Audit Office**.
Compulsory Competitive Tendering	Government policy requiring **local authorities** to offer selected services open to **competitive tender**. **Local authorities** which exceed the **de minimis** threshold are now having to put their housing management services through the **CCT** process.
compulsory purchase order	Decision by a **local authority**, confirmed by the relevant **Secretary of State**, under the Acquisition of Land Act 1981 to compulsorily acquire a property or land in the public interest, eg for the construction of a road or slum clearance.
concierge scheme	A staffed entrance service. Concierges are increasingly being used to make tower blocks safer and more desirable places to live. Although the costs of a concierge system, particularly if **CCTV** is employed, are high, reductions in the repairs and maintenance bill and increased rental income may make it economical in the long term.
conditions of engagement	Terms and conditions under which **contractors** are employed.
conditions of tenancy	The rights and obligations of the **tenant** and **landlord** contained in a **tenancy agreement**.
consent to dispose	Approval from a higher authority to sell land or property **assets**. In the case of **local authorities**, consent is needed from the **Secretary of State** whilst **registered social landlords** must obtain consent from the **national housing agency**.
conservation area	Designated area of special architectural or historic interest considered worthy of preservation. Once identified by a **local authority**, stringent planning requirements apply and additional grants may be available for the preservation or rehabilitation of properties.
Consolidated Fund	**Central government's** main expenditure and income account. It is held with the Bank of England.
Consolidation Bill	A **Bill** which brings several existing **Acts of Parliament** together into one (often with amendments) in order to simplify the statutes.
consortium	Group of organisations grouped together for a specific project. Consortia are formed to exploit **economies of scale** or share skills and abilities. The **Housing Finance Corporation** is a formalised mechanism for negotiating lower interest rates on borrowings by forming consortia of **housing associations**.
constant prices	See **real terms**.
Consumer Credit Licence	Licence required by any organisation providing credit. This includes **housing associations** offering **mortgages**.

contingency sum

Money set to one side and reserved to cover unforeseen losses or expenditure.

Continuous Recording of New Lettings

Monitoring system for new **housing associations** lettings, administered by **NFHA**. A questionnaire is filled in each time a new letting is made which records the type of house and household information such as income levels. A quarterly report is issued by the **NFHA,** summarising the national picture and each participating association receives a detailed annual analysis of their lettings. The **SFHA** run a similar scheme called **SCORE** and **WHATS** is the Welsh equivalent.

contract

Legal agreement between two or more parties. A **tenancy agreement** is one form of contract; the **landlord** allows the **tenant** to use the property and gets rent in return. Under **CCT** a contract describes the performance standards and service expected from a **contractor** and also includes methods of payment and procedures for enforcing compliance.

contract guarantee bond

See **surety bond.**

contract monitoring

System implemented by a **client** to record and respond to the performance of the **contractor** against specified targets.

contract packaging

Grouping services on a geographical or functional basis for the purpose of preparing and letting **contracts.**

contract standard

Standard of service delivery and performance outcomes outlined in a **contract.**

contract sum

The cost, set out in a **contract**, charged by a **contractor** for the delivery of a service or product. The **final account** may be higher once adjustments have been made.

contracting authority

Authority which is letting or planning to let a **contract**, ie the **client.**

contracting out

Process whereby services are delivered by external organisations rather than **in-house**, usually following a **tendering** procedure.

contractor

Organisation (or individual) which provides a service under a **contract**. In **CCT** the contractor has to bid for the award of the **contract.**

contributory

Welfare benefits which are only payable if the applicant has previously made sufficient National Insurance payments, eg **Unemployment Benefit** and **Incapacity Benefit.**

Control Total (or New Control Total)

Primary public spending measure used in the annual public expenditure planning round. It includes **general government** expenditure and external finance requirements of nationalised industries as well as the **capital expenditure** of **public corporations**. But it excludes privatisation receipts, **central government** debt interest and cyclical social security spending which are all regarded as outside the government's control.

Convention of Scottish Local Authorities	Representative body of Scottish **local authorities**.
conveyance	A legal document which **transfers** property which has **unregistered title** to a new owner.
co-operative housing association	A **housing association** which only provides or manages housing for the benefit of its **members**. Some co-ops only provide a housing management service for their **members** on behalf of the owner.
Co-ownership Scheme	When first established in 1964, the **Housing Corporation** provided loans for cost-rent schemes and co-ownership schemes which allowed residents to share in the increased market value of their homes on leaving. It was funded by a premium payment on the rent of in-coming co-owners. Many co-ownership societies have disbanded as co-owners have tended to take advantage of the **right to buy**.
Corporation Tax	A tax levied on the profits of UK companies. **Registered charities** are exempt and the **Secretary of State** for the Environment can refund the tax levied on the housing activities of **registered housing associations** under **Section 54** of the **Housing Act 1988**.
cost centre	A function or group of functions linked, for internal accounting purposes, to a **delegated budget**.
cost floor	An assessment of the original cost of developing and building a particular dwelling. This figure is used as a baseline which must be charged, under the **right to buy** scheme, for a dwelling.
cost rent	The rent which must be charged on a property to cover the costs of its construction, including the interest on any loans which were required and the costs of managing and maintaining the property. It represents the break even rent.
cost sale	The sale of properties at a break even price.
cost-benefit analysis	Procedure for analysing the performance of a programme on the basis of expenditure and likely incomes.
Council for the Protection of Rural England	A national charity which helps people protect their local countryside. **CPRE** seeks to provide well-researched, intelligent and practical solutions to problems which affect the English countryside.
Council of Ministers	The highest decision-making body of the European Union, the Council is made up of relevant ministers from the member states, for example the environment council includes the **Secretary of State** for the Environment plus his/her counterparts from other member states. The council deliberates and votes on directives proposed by the **European Commission**.
Council of Mortgage Lenders	The representative body of **mortgage** lending institutions. It is the sister organisation of the **BSA**.
Council of Welsh Districts	Welsh branch of the **Association of District Councils**. The Council has been merged with the Assembly of Welsh Counties to form the **Welsh Local Government Association**.

Council Tax	System of **local government** taxation which replaced the **Community Charge**. The tax is levied on households (not individuals) and is determined by the value of the property with a discount for single people.
county council	Elected municipal body responsible for county affairs in two-tier authorities in England & Wales. This includes education, strategic planning, highways and social services. Under the **Local Government Review**, as from April 1996 all Welsh county councils will be abolished and replaced by **unitary authorities**. Many in England will also change.
court order	Order of a court which must obeyed by any party to whom it is addressed. Where a court order is in the form of an **injunction** a party can be imprisoned or fined for failure to comply. Where the order is a **possession order** the order may be enforced by the court **bailiff** carrying out an **eviction**. Known as a **decree** in Scotland.
Credit Approval Transfer	A transfer of a **local authority credit approval** to a **housing association**, at which point it becomes actual cash.
credit approvals	**Central government** authorisation for a **local authority** to borrow money. **Local government** borrowing is restricted because it is considered to be public expenditure and is therefore counted in the **PSBR**. Approvals fall into two groups **Basic Credit Approvals** and **Supplementary Credit Approvals**. Also known as **permissions to borrow**.
credit union	Usually a locally-based savings scheme aimed at low income people with poor access to commercial financial organisations.
Crime Concern	National organisation working to support local crime prevention programmes such as Safer Cities and **Neighbourhood Watch**.
Crisis Loan	A discretionary interest free loan from the **Social Fund** available to anybody who needs help with one off expenses to prevent a crisis such as a fire, flood or loss of income.
critical path analysis	Analysis of steps or stages to be followed in a strategic approach to implementing change.
cross subsidy	Taking surpluses or gains from one area of activity to cover deficits or losses in another, eg English & Welsh **local authorities** have to cross-subsidise the **Housing Benefit** of poorer **tenants** out of the rental income from better off **tenants**.
current account	The account in which an organisation's non-capital transactions are recorded.
cyclical maintenance	Maintenance to the **housing stock** which is carried out periodically and forms part of the **planned maintenance** programme. The repairs can be of any size or cost, from roof repairs through to replacing a tap washer. For many large **landlords,** it is often more efficient to replace items periodically rather than in response to a complaint or breakage.

D

DCF	discounted cash flow
DEN 3	Domestic Energy Note 3
DFG	Disabled Facilities Grant
DHA	district health authority
DIYHO	Do-It-Yourself Homebuy Option
DIYSO	Do-It-Yourself Shared Ownership
DLA	Disability Living Allowance
DLO	direct labour organisation
DoE	Department of the Environment
DoH	Department of Health
DPC	Damp proof course. Incorporated into the walls of buildings in order to prevent damp rising from the ground.
DSO	direct services organisation
DSS	Department of Social Security
DTI	Department of Trade & Industry
DV	district valuer
damping formula	Device used by **central government** to limit the impact of year on year changes in entitlement to **credit approvals** and subsidies to **local authorities**.
date order system	A prioritisation system based upon length of waiting time, ie first come first served. **Local authorities** may prioritise some of their smaller repairs on such a basis, but **allocations** are usually decided on a **points system**.
day-to-day repairs	See **response maintenance**.
de minimis	Threshold below which **local authorities** are exempt from **CCT**. Set at £500,000 worth of **defined activities** pa for **HMCCT**, but the government is currently planning to reduce the de minimis threshold to 500 properties by 1999.
debt profile	Analysis of an organisation's borrowing. The profile shows the **principal**, the length of the repayment period and the interest to be charged.
decanting	Re-housing a **tenant** in order to carry out repairs or improvements to their home (or for demolition). The re-housing may be temporary or permanent.
decoration allowance	Money, vouchers or equipment provided by some **landlords** to enable a **tenant** to decorate their home.

decree	Scottish term for **court order**.
decree for possession	See **possession order**.
deed	A document signed by an individual, or on behalf of an organisation, where the person signing it records in the document that it is intended to be a **deed**. Prior to 1994, a **deed** had to be sealed by the person or organisation. A deed is statutorily required: • to transfer ownership of land • to **assign** a tenancy • to create a legally binding obligation to another person where that other person is not providing anything in return.
deed of postponement	Agreement by a lender, who is entitled to first claim on a borrower's **assets** in the event of default on a loan, that another lender can take first claim in their place.
deed of release	Agreement to release a **landlord** from legal responsibility for outstanding debts. It is usually used in a **stock transfer** where the legal responsibility for those debts is passed to the new **landlord** along with the properties.
default	Failure to comply with some requirement, usually an obligation imposed within a **contract**.
defect liability period	The time period, specified in a building **contract,** during which the **contractor** is liable for specific problems which may emerge. Usually 6 or 12 months.
defective dwelling	Properties which, because of their method of construction, are inherently structurally unsound and have been designated as a defective dwelling by the **Secretary of State**. Owners who purchased the dwellings from a **social housing landlord** prior to a date set out in regulations are entitled either to a grant to repair the property or to have the home bought back by the former **landlord**. Many types of prefabricated reinforced concrete houses are defective dwellings.
defensible space	A principle of crime prevention which promotes real or symbolic barriers on housing estates, with clearly defined areas of influence and opportunities for surveillance. The intention is to build self - regulating environments on four levels: • private – areas not visually or physically accessible to the public, eg inside the home • semi-private – areas under control of the occupant, but visually and physically accessible, eg the garden of a house • semi-public – area under control or within the area of responsibility of a specific group of occupants, eg hallways of multi-occupancy flats • public space – area of space to which the public has access by right, eg a road. Defensible space attempts to *privatise* as much area in an estate as possible, this is often achieved by developing buffer areas around houses through enclosed front and rear gardens, replacing open spaces with communal facilities such as play areas.

deferred interest mortgage	A loan on which the borrower only pays part of the initial interest, the remainder is added to the **principal** and interest is, in turn, charged upon it.
deferred shared ownership	A mechanism whereby participants in **low cost home-ownership** schemes rent their property on a short-term **tenancy** whilst, for example, their existing home is being sold.
deficit funding	Finance which is provided for certain costs after they have been incurred.
defined activity	Some of the functions included in housing management which are set out in regulations and which must be submitted to **CCT** if they exceed the **de minimis** threshold.
delegated budget	Budget for an item of expenditure within which spending decisions are able to be made locally, eg by an area manager or (in **CCT**) a **contractor**. See also **cost centre**.
delict	Scottish equivalent of **tort**.
demolition order	Order made by a **local authority** directed to the owner of a dwelling or **house in multiple occupation** requiring its demolition because it is **Unfit for Human Habitation**.
density	A measure of how crowded a property, or area, is. Density is calculated by the number of residents (or households) in a given area, eg an hectare or square metre for a single property.
Department of Health	**Central government** department with responsibility for the National Health Service.
Department of National Heritage	Government department with responsibility, among other things, for **listing buildings**.
Department of Social Security	**Central government** department with responsibility for **social security benefits**, such as **Income Support**, **Unemployment Benefit** and the **Social Fund**. Although it does not have direct responsibility for **Housing Benefit** payments and adjudication, it does set out the regulations which cover its administration. Social security issues for the whole of the UK are dealt with by the **DSS**.
Department of the Environment	**Central government** department with responsibility for **local government**, housing, urban regeneration, planning and environmental protection in England.
Department of Trade & Industry	**Central government** department with responsibility for trade policy, export promotion, energy, corporate and consumer affairs and industry. The **DTI** also administers the **Energy Design Advice Scheme**.
depreciation	A reflection of the reduction in value of an **asset** over time. Usually the value of an **asset** is cut each year in an organisation's accounts by dividing the original cost by its expected life span.
Derelict Land Grant	Funding programme to reclaim derelict land damaged by industrial or other uses that cannot be used without being treated. Grants are

paid direct to land owners and are determined by the **district valuer**. This scheme has now been folded into the operations of **English Partnerships**.

design & build contract	**Development** process where the **client** employs a single **contractor** to oversee both the design and building of a project.
designated stress area	**Local authority** area with high levels of social deprivation and poor quality physical infrastructure. These areas qualify for extra resources from **central government**.
developer	Organisation or individual specialising in the **development** process. A developer organises one or more of the following: land acquisition, the architects role, the planning function and the actual construction.
development	Term used to describe the building or the physical change in use of any building or land.
development agent	An organisation providing an expertise in the management of the **development** process. Many smaller **housing associations** employ **secondary housing associations** in this capacity.
development plan	Document outlining the **local authority's** planning policies and proposals for **development** in its area. These can be **structure plans**, **local plans** or **unitary development plans**.
difficult to let	See **hard to let**.
direct access accommodation	Emergency **hostel** type accommodation usually providing a temporary roof for single rough sleepers.
direct deductions	See **direct payments**.
direct labour organisation	**Local authority** department which provides manual labour for municipal projects.
direct payments	Welfare benefit deductions collected by the **Benefits Agency** and paid to a third party, eg for gas, water, electricity or **rent arrears**. Known as **direct deductions** in Northern Ireland.
direct services organisation	Generic term for a **local government** department which provides some form of service to **clients**, eg the housing service. Sometimes used in the context of the **in-house team** in a **CCT tendering** process.
Directive	A piece of **EU** legislation which requires a member state (eg the United Kingdom) to amend its own law to implement agreed **EU** objectives. The member state has discretion in the choice of how to bring about the change and its actual form. Directives can, in some cases, be enforced against public bodies and some highly regulated private organisations.
directors & officers insurance	Insurance covering **board members** and officers of a **housing association** from claims of wrongful acts. The **NFHA** arranges block cover for its members.
Disability Discrimination Act 1995	Introduced new measures aimed at bringing discrimination against disabled people to an end. Among other areas the Act covers the purchase and renting of land and property.

Disability Living Allowance	**Non-means tested, non-contributory social security benefit** equivalent to **Attendance Allowance**, but for under 65 year olds with personal care or supervision needs. **DLA** has an additional component to cover mobility needs.
Disability Working Allowance	A **social security benefit** similar to **Family Credit** but for claimants who are disabled.
Disabled Facilities Grant	A mandatory **means tested** grant available to **owner-occupiers** and **tenants** from **local authorities**. The grant covers the cost of **adaptations** needed by disabled occupants to remain in their own homes up to a limit of £20,000. Under the **Housing Grants, Construction & Regeneration Act 1996**, DFG continues to be mandatory, whilst all the other renovation grants become discretionary.
discount bonds	Bonds purchased at below their **redemption yield**, in return the borrower has to repay more than they initially received.
discounted cash flow	Accounting tool for showing future cash flows at current prices (**net present value**). Based on the notion that cash reduces in value over time because it could otherwise have been earning interest. Money is discounted using interest rates, which represent the **opportunity cost** of not investing in **gilts**.
dispersed hostel	A series of geographically separate **supported housing** projects which are serviced by a single **warden** facility.
disregard	Income which is ignored when calculating the resources of a claimant for a **means tested** welfare benefit.
district auditor	Local representative of the **Audit Commission**.
district council	Elected municipal body responsible for housing, planning, economic development and tourism in two-tier authorities. As from April 1996 all Scottish & Welsh district councils will be abolished and replaced by **unitary authorities**. Many in England will also change.
district council (Northern Ireland)	**District councils** in Northern Ireland only have responsibility for entertainment, culture, recreation, environmental health, cleansing and sanitation, cemeteries and markets. Several other services are vested with **area boards** but housing is the responsibility of the **Northern Ireland Housing Executive**.
district health authority	Public body with responsibility for purchasing health services within a health district. There are 143 **DHA**s in England, 9 in Wales and 13 **Health Boards** in Scotland plus 4 Health & Social Services **Area Boards** in Northern Ireland. They have responsibility for providing a strategic framework for improving health levels within their district, often in conjunction with other agencies, such as **local authority** housing departments and **housing associations**.
district valuer	Person appointed by **central government** to advise public bodies on the value of property.

disturbance payments	Payment made to the occupier of a property who has to move out because of:
	• improvements
	• redevelopment work
	• a **closing order**
	• or a **demolition order**.
	The payment should cover the **reasonable** expenses incurred in moving home. In some cases, payments are mandatory but there is also a power to make discretionary payments where the occupier does not qualify for mandatory payments. Occupants may also be entitled to **home-loss payments**.
Do-It-Yourself Homebuy Option	A DIY version of the **Homebuy Option** scheme available in Wales.
Do-It-Yourself Shared Ownership	A **Housing Corporation** and **Tai Cymru** scheme to assist **housing associations** purchase property on behalf of individuals who then enter into a **shared ownership** agreement with the association.
Domestic Energy Note 3	**DoE** document defining which **housing association** homes qualify for **HAG** to cover the cost of replacing heating systems and providing new insulation.
dowry	Within a **stock transfer**, the properties may be in such poor condition that the **catch-up repair** bill exceeds the total value of the properties. Under such circumstances the **local authority** may pay a dowry to the receiving organisation to facilitate the **transfer**.
dry run	Process of checking **CCT** systems particularly the bidding and tender evaluation process.
dualities of interest	Situations where a **housing association board member** has a personal interest in a decision he or she is being asked to make. The interests of the individual **board member** and the **housing association** may conflict, which may lead to a decision which is not in the association's best interests. Sections 13 and 15 of the **Housing Associations Act 1985** limit the material and financial payments to **housing association board members** and staff (including members of their family) plus any company of which they are a director. **Housing association** rules will also usually set out the procedures to be followed when a duality of interest arises. The **national housing agencies** closely monitor adherence to these rules.

EAGA	See **Eaga Ltd**
EC	European Community
ECSC	**European Coal & Steel Communities programme**
EDAS	**Energy Design Advice Scheme**
EEO	**Energy Efficiency Office**
EHA	**Empty Homes Agency**
EHCS	**English House Condition Survey**
EMAS	**Eco-Management & Audit Scheme**
EMB	**Estate Management Board**
EPU	**empty property unit**
ERCF	**Estates Renewal Challenge Fund**
ERDF	**European Regional Development Fund**
ESF	**European Structural Fund** or **European Social Fund**.
EU	European Union.
EZ	**Enterprise Zone**
Eaga Ltd	Private non-profit distributing organisation which administers the government's **Home Energy Efficiency Scheme**. Its sister company Eaga Services Ltd administers **energy efficiency** schemes with electricity companies and **local authorities** across the country. Formerly known as the Energy Action Grants Agency.
Ealing Judgment	A landmark court judgment which brought into question the wider welfare role of housing managers beyond mere property management.
earnings arrestment	Scottish term for **attachment of earnings**.
eco-audit	See **environmental audit**.
Eco-Management & Audit Scheme	A system of **environmental audit** developed by the **Department of the Environment** and **local authority associations**. It tailored the European Community's voluntary **EMAS**, designed for private business, to the needs of **local government**. The scheme's requirements are:

1) a policy stating the organisation's environmental aims (particularly those which exceed the statutory minimum)
2) a review of the environmental impact of its activities
3) a programme to achieve the objectives of its policy goals
4) a management system which defines responsibilities, procedures and tools
5) periodic audits to assess progress
6) a published statement of environmental performance
7) external verification of the process and validation of the public statement.

economic rent	Level of rent which needs to be charged to cover the long-run costs of supplying the dwelling.
economic subsidy	The gap between the **economic rent** and the **actual rent**.
economies of scale	Cost savings which an organisation makes as a direct result of the size of its operations. The per unit costs incurred on many activities will be lower for larger organisations, eg larger **landlords** should have a lower average management cost per **unit**. Of course, the opposite may occur, a phenomenon known as diseconomies of scale.
eligible for assistance	Statutory term in the **Housing Act 1996** applied to individuals who are **homeless**. Only those eligible for assistance are entitled to any assistance from a **local authority**. The **Act** allows the **Secretary of State** to issue **Statutory Instruments** setting out who is ineligible for assistance because they are **persons from abroad**. An **asylum seeker** is ineligible for assistance if they have any accommodation in the United Kingdom, however temporary.
eligible rent	Used in **Housing Benefit** to determine that part of the gross weekly rent which represents payment for the right to occupy the property, eg any water rates and heating costs etc. do not form part of the eligible rent.
eligible residential property	Dwellings which can be financed by **HITs**. They must be: • empty properties or currently let on **assured shorthold tenancies** • **freehold** or long-**lease** (21 years or more) at low rent • costing less than £125,000 in central London and £85,000 elsewhere • and, subsequently let on an **assured shorthold** basis.
eligible staff	Staff entitled to compensation and redundancy payments following the letting of a **contract**. Governed by the Employment Protection (Consolidation) Act 1978.
Empty Homes Agency	The **EHA** is currently funded by government, the property profession and housing charities to bring empty housing into use for those in need. The agency works with owners, professional advisors and investors as well as **housing associations** and **local authorities** which have adopted an **empty property strategy**.
empty property strategy	A **landlord's** policy for dealing with empty properties.
empty property unit	Section which may exist within a **local authority** housing department with strategic responsibility for minimising the level of **voids** within the **local authority** area as well as in the authority's own stock.
enabling role	Facilitating the provision of new or improved housing through the activities of others, eg a **local authority** setting a framework for and promoting the activities of **housing associations** and private developers.
endowment mortgage	Form of **mortgage** in which the **mortgagor** pays interest to the **mortgagee** but makes no direct repayments on the **principal**. In the meantime a monthly premium payment is made to an endowment policy which matures when repayment of the **principal** is due.

The **mortgagor** keeps any excess money which the policy delivers over the cost of the property, but is also responsible for making up any shortfall.

Energy Action Scotland	Organisation which promotes **energy efficiency**, **energy conservation** and affordable warmth in Scotland.
energy conservation	See **energy efficiency**.
Energy Design Advice Scheme	**DTI** scheme which provides a free low energy design consultancy covering new and refurbished housing.
energy efficiency	Often used interchangeably with **energy conservation**. Its strict definition is the provision of a given amount of energy (heat, light or power) from the minimum amount of energy input, through a variety of techniques and technologies. It is also sometimes used to refer to reductions in energy waste. Energy efficiency of dwellings is measured by a number of standards, two of the most common being **NHER** and **Starpoint**.
Energy Efficiency Office	Section within the **DoE** with responsibility for promoting **energy efficiency**.
enforcement notice	A notice served by the local planning authority where there has been a breach of planning controls. It sets out the nature of the violation, the steps required to remedy it and the date by which these steps must be taken.
English Heritage	Government body responsible for over 400 national monuments. Advises the **DoE** on planning where conservation is an issue and the **Department of National Heritage** on **listed buildings**.
English House Condition Survey	**DoE** sponsored survey conducted every 5 years to investigate the physical condition of housing in England. The **EHCS** considers a sample of dwellings in England and reports on the age of the stock, house design, **tenure** profile, **overcrowding** and **unfit dwellings**. Similar surveys are carried out in the rest of the UK.
English Nature	Government body responsible for advising the government on nature conservation including the identification of **Sites of Special Scientific Interest**. Formerly the Nature Conservancy Council for England.
English Partnerships	Government agency set up in 1994 to promote job creation, inward investment and environmental improvement through land reclamation by supporting partnerships between **local authorities**, the private sector and voluntary bodies. It replaced the **Derelict Land Grant**, City Grant and English Estates. It provides advice to prospective partners, enters into joint ventures, provides loans and guarantees, gap funding and may become involved in direct development. Also known as the **Urban Regeneration Agency**.
Enterprise Zones	A **DoE** scheme to remove certain financial and administrative burdens from businesses. The principal benefits being exemption from rates, tax breaks on **capital expenditure** and a greatly simplified planning regime. **EZ** status lasts for 10 years, however, no new zones are currently planned.

enveloping	Co-ordinated external repairs to a block or group of properties, especially in inner city areas. Also known as **block repairs** or **group repair**.
Environment & Social Affairs Select Committee, EC (Sub Committee C)	House of Lords **Select Committee** with a remit to investigate and report on activities and issues for which the **Department of the Environment** is responsible.
Environment Select Committee	House of Commons **Select Committee** with remit to investigate and report on activities and issues for which the **Department of the Environment** is responsible.
environmental audit	Process of reviewing and evaluating an organisation's environmental performance as measured against established goals, objectives and targets. The **audit** should seek to improve performance and be periodic, systematic, objective and documented.
environmental improvements	Activities designed to improve the local surroundings, eg park space and pavements, brick cleaning and traffic calming.
Environmental Protection Act 1990	Outlines the law relating to **statutory nuisance** and **abatement notices**.
equal opportunities policy	Strategy to ensure equal access to employment and services. Under the Race Relations Act 1976 **landlords** cannot discriminate on racial grounds as an employer or as a provider or manager of housing services. The Sex Discrimination Act 1975 prevents **landlords** from discriminating in relation to employment or the provision of goods, facilities and services by treating a person less favourably than another on the grounds of their sex and not to discriminate against married persons in the field of employment. The Equal Pay Act 1970 further requires them not to discriminate in respect of pay and conditions of employment. Many organisations' equal opportunities policy goes beyond the minimum legal requirements.
equity	Residual value of an organisation's **assets** after all its **liabilities** have been allowed for. When used in the context of a **mortgage** or loan, equity is the money which would be left over if the **asset** was sold and the outstanding debt repaid.
equity sharing	Joint ownership of **equity**. In **shared ownership** schemes, the equity is shared between the owner (usually a **local authority** or **housing association)** and the occupant.
Estate Action	DoE administered scheme which provided **capital expenditure** resources to English **local authorities** and **Housing Action Trusts** through **credit approvals** for renovating run-down housing estates. Estate Action also aimed to improve estate management. The programme is now defunct and its funds are now being diverted into the **Single Regeneration Budget**.
Estate Management Board	A **TMO** which works in partnership with the **local authority**. The board is usually made up of **tenant** representatives, councillors, and other co-opted members, although **tenants** are usually in the majority. Alternatively, **TMOs** can take the form of a **Tenant Management Co-operative**.

Estates Renewal Challenge Fund	A competitive funding system set up by the **DoE** in December 1995 to distribute resources for the transfer of **local authority** housing to new **landlords**. It is hoped that **ERCF** will extend the **stock transfer** movement to urban areas which have higher investment requirements and poor **asset** cover, ie the value of the properties is often insufficient to provide cover for the required levels of borrowing.
ethnic monitoring	Systematic collection of data on the provision of services to ethnic minority groups to ensure the organisation's **equal opportunities policy** is being fulfilled.
European Coal & Steel Communities programme	A European Union fund which provides fixed 1% loans to individuals and organisations to purchase or rehabilitate housing as well as financing retraining and resettlement schemes. The scheme is under-subscribed, but 50% of beneficiaries must be working miners.
European Commission	Executive arm of the European Union. The Commission comprises a number of commissioners from member states and has the power to propose legislation to the **Council of Ministers** and monitor the implementation of **Directives**.
European Parliament	The Parliament is a directly elected body of **MEPs** but only has the power to amend legislation and is largely viewed as a consultative body at present.
European Regional Development Fund	A **European Structural Fund** targeted on those areas: • whose **GDP** falls well below the European Union average (Objective 1) • with a declining industrial base (Objective 2) • where rural development is necessary because of declining investment in agriculture (Objective 5b). Many areas in the UK qualify under one of these objectives and housing projects may be incorporated into projects receiving **ERDF** funding. The **ERDF** is administered in the UK by the **DTI** whilst the regional allocation is managed by the **IROs**.
European Social Fund	A **European Structural Fund** which provides **revenue expenditure** to combat long-term unemployment of people aged over 25 and to integrate people under 25 into the job market. The money is not targeted on areas but on people with employment difficulties. Between 1991 and 1992, the UK received the highest **ESF** allocation of all member states. **Local authorities** receive around 25% of the allocation, the voluntary sector receives 15% and **central government** keeps the rest to fund initiatives such as the Youth Training Scheme. Although **ESF** funds could be used to train construction workers until the early 1990s it is now difficult to attract such money for housing orientated projects.
European Structural Fund	A series of funds available from the European Union to mitigate the effects of the Single Market. The funds are targeted at regions and social groups under the five objectives of: 1) improving economic health of the regions whose development is lagging behind 2) helping areas affected by serious industrial decline 3) combating long-term unemployment of people aged over 25 4) integrating people under 25 into the job market

5) adjusting agricultural structures and developing rural areas. The **European Regional Development Fund** and the **European Social Fund** are examples.

Eurorex

A French inter-ministerial body which encourages collaboration between French housing and construction bodies and those working in other European countries to stimulate research and development.

evaluation framework

Tool for evaluating possible **client-contractor splits** against specific criteria such as flexibility, costs and customer satisfaction.

eviction

The physical removal of occupants from a property. In all but very limited exceptions, occupants can only be evicted from a dwelling by the county court **bailiff** enforcing a **court order**.

exceptions policy

A facility sanctioned by **PPG 3** which allows English **local authorities** to approve the **development** of **affordable housing** schemes which fall outside the area's **development plan**. For such a **development** to proceed the local planning authority must demonstrate the existence of a need for the properties. They usually occur on sites adjacent to existing built up rural areas and enable the land to be acquired at below the prevailing market value.

exclusive possession

The right to occupy one's home on the basis that you can exclude the **landlord** and other persons except in limited circumstances, eg where the **landlord** has the occasional right to enter and view the premises to look at the state of repair. All **tenants** have the right of exclusive possession; most **licensees** do not.

executive agency

Any government body charged with executive powers to provide certain public services, eg the **Benefits Agency**, **BRE** and the Prison Service.

exempt charity

A charitable organisation which is not registered with the **Charity Commission**. These charities are **Industrial and Provident Societies** and as such are registered under the Industrial & Provident Societies Act 1965. Whilst they are exempt from most of the control exerted by the **Charity Commission** over registered charities, they may seek advice from the Commission and obtain indemnity in certain circumstances.

exempt dwelling

A property on which no **Council Tax** is payable. This includes student households and certain empty dwellings, eg dwellings which fail the **fitness standard**.

exit strategy

An outline plan of the way in which an organisation will pull out of a project at some future specified date. The strategy usually describes how the aims and methods of the programme will continue after funding stops and the delivery organisations have left.

exit survey

Survey of client satisfaction conducted with **tenants** leaving housing offices.

external audit

An **audit** carried out by an impartial, external organisation which acts as a verification of the organisation's **internal audit**.

FBHO	**Federation of Black Housing Organisations**
FEANSTA	The European Federation of National Organisations Working with the Homeless. FEANSTA's objective is the elimination of homelessness in Europe.
FFY	**Foyer Federation for Youth**
FMPR	**Financial Management and Policy Review**
FOS	**Flats Over Shops**
factoring	A Scottish term to describe the employment of a third party to perform certain property management functions. Originally used in connection with rent collection, but factors often have responsibility for repairs etc. Some **local authorities** perform a factoring role, particularly for those properties sold under the **right to buy**.
Fair Rent	This is a rent set by the **rent officer** and is only applicable to **protected tenancies** and pre-1989 **housing association** tenancies, ie not **assured tenancies**. It is also known as a **Registered Rent**. Once set, it is the maximum rent which a **landlord** can charge for that particular property under a **regulated tenancy**.
Family Allowance	See **Child Benefit**.
Family Credit	A **means tested, social security benefit** for low income people who work over 16 hours per week and have children.
feasibility study	A study into the feasibility of a project within resource and time constraints. Feasibility studies often focus upon the financial aspects of a project but may look into any of the relevant factors involved.
Federation of Black Housing Organisations	Member body of housing organisations working to improve the lives of black and other minority ethnic people in **housing need**. FBHO lobbies policy makers and provides information, training, consultancy, research, advice and support services.
feu duty	Cash payment from the owner of a land or property to the original feudal superior. Since the Land Tenure Reform (Scotland) Act 1974, feu duties are aggregated and paid in a one-off sum by the purchaser and the obligation is extinguished thereafter.
fidelity guarantee	An insurance policy against costs incurred as a result of an employee's fraud or dishonesty.
final account	The final cost charged by a building **contractor**. Based on the **contract sum** with adjustments for unforeseen costs incurred during the project. Also known as **out-turn costs**.
final certificate	Notification from the architect that the building work is complete. The final certificate is the notification for the client to release the **retention sum** after the **defect liability period** has expired.
Finance Act 1996	As announced in the 1995 Budget, this **Act** introduced a system of tax incentives to encourage the development of **Housing Investment Trusts**.

Financial Management and Policy Review

Regular government scrutiny of **non-departmental public bodies** (**quangos**). The exercise assesses the continuing justification and need for a particular body on policy grounds and considers the adequacy of their systems of financial management and control. The **Housing Corporation** is normally reviewed every five years, the last time being early 1995. The first stage of the review is known as the **Prior Options Study**.

financial modelling

Process of checking the viability of a project under different financial scenarios, eg different interest rates, inflation levels, rental income etc.

financial objective

Rate of return specified by the **Secretary of State** which the **DSO/HCU** must attain to win a **CCT contract**.

financial viability returns

An assurance from a **housing association** to the **national housing agency** that the financial risks involved in a project can be covered by the association. Such an assurance is essential before the **national housing agency** provides **HAG** for a project.

First Reading

Formal notification to the Houses of Parliament of a proposed **Bill**. It acts as the House's order to print the **Bill**.

fitness standard

Generic name for the physical standards which dwellings must meet for them not to be classified as **Unfit for Human Habitation** or **Below the Tolerable Standard** (in Scotland).

fixed term tenancy

Any **tenancy** which is time limited, ie 6 months. Alternatively a **tenancy** may be **periodic**.

Flats Over Shops

DoE initiative which aimed to bring under-used property over shops into use. The programme provides **Supplementary Credit Approvals** for **local authorities** to support schemes through **LAHAG**. The scheme was inspired by **Living Over The Shop**.

flexible tenure

General term for **shared ownership** schemes in which the occupant can **staircase** their **equity share** according to their needs and circumstances. Flexible tenure has also been used to describe occupants moving from one form of **tenure**, eg **owner-occupation** to another, eg **social housing** whilst remaining in the same property.

Flexible Tenure for the Elderly

A **housing association equity sharing** model available in Wales and aimed at elderly people.

floating support

Variable support given to people on a peripatetic basis. In some cases there may be an element of **pre-tenancy** or pre-occupation support and a wide range of support may be offered depending on the particular project.

flush threshold

Doorways etc. without a sill making them wheelchair accessible.

forfeiture

The termination of a **fixed term tenancy** because of a breach of the **conditions of tenancy** by the **tenant**, eg failure to pay rent for a stated time period. The **tenancy agreement** must contain a **right of re-entry**.

former tenants' arrears	Unpaid rent on **tenancies** which have been terminated. After a period they are written off as **bad debts** if they remain unrecovered. Also known as **past tenants' arrears**.
foyer	A housing project which provides a home, support and training for employment to homeless people between the ages of 16 and 25. They tend to be one-off projects financed by **HAG, local authority** funds, private finance and other voluntary sources.
Foyer Federation for Youth	The Foyer Federation exists to support and develop a national network of **foyers** – providing affordable accommodation with access to training, education and employment opportunities.
freehold	Description of a **tenure** of land or buildings. Owning the freehold is equivalent to outright permanent ownership though technically all land in the UK is owned by the Crown. The owner of the freehold can grant **leases** or **tenancies** either for a specific length of time, eg 99 years, or on a periodic basis, eg weekly or monthly. The owner can set out the conditions of the **lease** or **tenancy** and receives rent.
friendly society	A mutual, but unincorporated organisation registered with the **Registrar of Friendly Societies**. Although many **housing associations** are also registered with the **Registrar of Friendly Societies**, they are in fact **Industrial and Provident Societies**.
Friends of the Earth	Pressure group which campaigns on environmental issues, including **energy efficiency** in housing.
front loading	Phenomenon whereby interest payments are greatest in the earlier stages of repaying a debt.
fuel poverty	Inability to achieve affordable warmth because of poor levels of **energy efficiency** in the home. Although financial hardship plays a role, increases in income alone are not sufficient to alleviate fuel poverty; poor insulation and inefficient heating systems are the root cause.
fully mutual housing association	An association which only provides homes for its **members**, ie in order to become a **tenant** one has to become a **member**. **Co-operative housing associations** are generally fully mutual.
functional audit	Process of assessing organisational performance particularly focusing on the provision of **defined activities**.

GAA	general allocation area
GDP	**Gross Domestic Product**
GGFD	**General Government Financial Deficit**
GIA	**General Improvement Area**
GLC	**Greater London Council**
GNI	**Generalised Needs Index**
GOR	**Government Offices for the Regions**

Garden City
Late-Victorian idea promoted by Ebenezer Howard to combine the values of the countryside with those of the town. New towns were designed on **green field sites** funded by investors purchasing farm land which would rise in value as the town expanded.

gearing
This term is used in a variety of contexts. In accountancy it refers to an organisation's ratio of debt to **equity**, but in other arenas it refers to the ratio of public to private money. Also known as **leverage**.

general allocation area
Term used in the **allocation** of **social housing** in Northern Ireland to classify the first choice preference estate selected by the potential **tenant**. Any offer made in that **GAA** is considered to be **reasonable**.

General Fund
Main **local authority** fund from which most services are financed.

General Fund contribution
A transfer of funds from the **General Services Fund** to the **Housing Revenue Account**. As in England, Scottish **HRAs** are now **ring-fenced** to prevent such contributions.

General Fund transfer
Transfer of money from the **HRA** to the **General Fund**. Authorities not in receipt of **HRA subsidy** must pay a notional negative subsidy into the **General Fund** from their **HRA**, but other transfers are banned because the **HRA** is **ring-fenced**.

general government
Broad definition of the government sector used in national accounts, includes **central government** and **local government**.

General Government Financial Deficit
Internationally accepted measure of the balance between **general government** expenditure and revenue.

General Improvement Area
An area of poor quality housing in England or Wales which qualified for increased grants and subsidised environmental improvements. They were a precursor to **renewal areas**.

General Services Fund
Scottish term for the **General Fund**.

Generalised Needs Index
Compound measure of relative **housing need** used by the **Department of the Environment** to calculate a **local authority's** ACG. As from 1996/7 each authority's **HIP allocation** will be determined through a competitive process but **GNI** will still be used to determine the regional allocation.

gentrification	Renovation of previously run-down inner city areas as a result of inward investment, which then become inhabited by **owner-occupiers** rather than **tenants**, wealthier households rather than poorer ones and younger people rather than older people.
gilts	Gilt-edged securities of fixed interest issued by the **central government**, generally seen as the safest form of investment. The rate of return on a gilt-edged bond acts as a base around which other financial services are charged.
Giro rent collection	Method of collecting rent which is aimed at ensuring the safety of rent collectors. The scheme allows **tenants** to pay their rent at the Post Office through the Giro Bank, avoiding the need for a home visit.
golden share	A form of veto shareholding which allows a party to prevent an organisation from pursuing certain courses of action, eg **local authorities** may seek a golden share in any **local housing companies** set up from their **housing stock**.
governing instrument	The constitution of a **housing association** or a company.
Government Offices for the Regions	Series of **central government** offices which administer European and UK government funding programmes throughout England such as **Estate Action, City Challenge, Urban Programme, Housing Investment Programme, TEC** funding, education-business links, Regional Enterprise Grants, Regional Selective Assistance and **European Structural Funds**. Activities of the **Department of Environment, Trade & Industry**, Education & Employment, and Transport are all incorporated in **GOR**s. The regions represented by an office are North West, Yorkshire & Humberside, North East, West Midlands, East Midlands, Merseyside, Eastern, South West, South East and London. Also known as **IROs**.
grant aided repairs	A small part of the **ADP** in Wales allocated by **Tai Cymru** to **housing associations** for exceptional repairs.
grant-aided land	Land owned by a **housing association** which cannot be disposed of without prior consent from the **national housing agency** because it was bought or developed with the aid of public subsidies or loans.
Grants for Renting and Ownership	See **GRO grants**.
Greater London Council	Former **local authority** for the whole of Greater London. Abolished on 1/5/86 under the Local Government Act 1985.
green belt	An area where **development** is restricted in order to prevent urban sprawl encroaching into the countryside. They are designated in **local authorities' structure plans** but the detailed boundaries are defined in **local plans**.
green field site	A **development** location which has not previously been built on, as opposed to a **brown field site**.
Green Paper	Consultative document outlining the government's views on an issue of concern. May be followed by a **White Paper** leading to legislation.

greenhouse effect	Phenomenon whereby certain gases trap solar heat in the atmosphere. It is a natural process which maintains the earth's temperature but current increases in carbon dioxide and other greenhouse gases are likely to magnify the process resulting in global warming.
GRO grants	**Grants for Renting and Ownership**. Money from within the **Scottish Homes' ADP** which is targeted at **developers** and non-**registered housing associations** to provide **low cost home-ownership** and rented accommodation at **market rents**.
Gross Domestic Product	A measure of the total flow of goods and services produced by a national economy.
ground rent	Rent paid by a **leaseholder** to the **freeholder**. Also known as **chief rent**.
grounds for possession	Legal term to describe the grounds on which a **landlord** may be granted a **possession order** for a dwelling. These grounds are set out for England & Wales in statute, eg for **secure tenants** in England & Wales they are set out in the **Housing Act 1985**.
group home	Shared living project where single people live together as a single household within the context of a special project, eg a drugs rehabilitation scheme.
group repair	See **enveloping**.
guideline rent increase	A **DoE** assessment of how much a **local authority** needs to increase its rents in order to balance its notional **HRA** whilst still providing a standard level of service. Since 1996 any **actual rent** increases which exceed the guideline rent increase will not receive **Rent Rebate** subsidy on the excess.

HA	housing association
HAA	Housing Action Area
HACT	Housing Associations Charitable Trust
HAG	Housing Association Grant
HALS	Housing Association Leasing Scheme
HAMA	Housing Associations as Managing Agents
HAMA Plus	**HAMA** type scheme which focuses on bringing empty private sector properties which are in need of repair back into use.
HAMIA	Housing Association Mutual Insurance Association
HAPM	Housing Association Property Mutual
HARP	Homes Above Retail Premises
HAT	Housing Action Trust
HATOS	Housing Association Tenants Ombudsman Service
HBF	House Builders' Federation
HC	Housing Corporation
HCT	Housing Centre Trust
HCU	housing contractor unit
HEES	Home Energy Efficiency Scheme
HFC	Housing Finance Corporation (The)
HIP	See **Housing Investment Programme (allocation)**
HIT	Housing Investment Trust
HIV+	See **AIDS**.
HMCCT	Housing Management CCT
HMO	house in multiple occupation
HMP	Housing Market Package
HNI	Housing Needs Index
HOMES	Housing Organisations Mobility and Exchange Services
HRA	Housing Revenue Account
HRS	Home Release Scheme
HSG	Housing Support Grant

Habitat II	United Nations world conference on human settlements in Istanbul June 1996. Key themes were **sustainable development** and adequate shelter for all. Also known as **City Summit**.
Habitual Residence Test	An assessment of an applicant's eligibility for a **means tested** welfare benefit which determines whether their normal home is in the UK.
HAR 10	Annual return to the **Housing Corporation** made by all **registered social landlords** in England detailing statistical information such as staffing levels, the **housing stock**, sales and **stock transfers**, lettings, **hostels**, private sector finance, management, rent collection, repairs and **voids**.
HAR 14	The performance standards monitoring form which all **registered social landlords** in England must complete and return to the **Housing Corporation** annually. It covers information on the type of **housing needs** the association meets, its **board of management**, financial management, housing management, maintenance and **development**.
harassment	Behaviour deliberately intended to intimidate, dominate or harm an individual or a certain group, such as members of minority ethnic communities.
hard to let	A property for which the **landlord** cannot readily find a **tenant**. Usually due to poor condition of the house itself or the estate or because its design renders it unsuitable for many households in **housing need**, eg high rise flats. There is no statutory definition of hard to let, so usage tends to vary across **local authorities** and **housing associations**. **Local authorities** have to provide some figure of hard to let properties in their stock for their **HIP** returns. Also known as **difficult to let**.
HA Weekly	See *Housing Associations Weekly*.
head-lease	See **head-tenancy**.
head-tenancy	A **tenancy** between a **landlord** and a **tenant** in which the **tenant** is actually **sub-letting** the property to another **tenant**. The **tenancy** between the two **tenants** is known as the **sub-tenancy**. Also known as a **head-lease**.
Health Board	Scottish equivalent of a **Regional Health Authority**.
highways agreements	Agreement from a developer that roads and footpaths will be included in a **development** project. Management of the roads and footpaths will revert to the local highway authority once construction is complete.
HIP returns	Statement supplied by English **local authorities** to the **DoE** about the **housing stock** in its area and its investment plans for the coming year. This includes information about the age of the stock, **tenure**, the type of housing (including **special needs housing** provision, tower blocks, **hostels** etc.), **hard to let** properties, **voids**, **unfitness**, **energy efficiency** ratings, **waiting lists**, **referrals**, **tenancy turnover** and **homeless** households. The information provided by the **local authority** is used, in part, to calculate the **GNI** which is then

considered when allocating **Housing Investment Programme credit approvals**.

Historic Buildings Council for Wales	Advisory **quango** to **Secretary of State** for Wales on the use and preservation of historic buildings.
HM Land Registry	Government agency with responsibility for administering the registration of title to (ownership of) land. Registration of title is compulsory on sales throughout England & Wales. The equivalent function is carried out in Scotland by **Registers of Scotland**.
Home Energy Efficiency Scheme	Grants scheme funded by the **Department of the Environment's Energy Efficiency Office** and administered by **Eaga Ltd**. The scheme provides grants for loft insulation, draught-proofing and advice on energy saving in homes of people on low-incomes and aged 60 or over. Installers must be accredited by **Eaga Ltd.**
home improvement agency	A non-profit making body offering independent advice and support to help older people, people with disabilities and other low income households to repair, improve or adapt their homes. The service they provide ranges from small-scale repairs to major works and includes advice, advocacy and project management.

home loss payments

Statutory payments to occupiers who are forced to move from their home as a result of:

- a **compulsory purchase order**, a demolition or a **closing order**
- an undertaking given by a **landlord** not to use part of the property for human habitation
- displacement by a **local authority** which has previously acquired the land and now wishes to develop or improve it
- in the case of a **housing association tenant**, permanent displacement due to the improvement of the dwelling or redevelopment of the land
- the making of a **possession order** under certain **grounds for possession** contained in the **Housing Act 1985**.

The **tenant** must have been in occupation of the property for at least a year before the displacement to qualify for payments. If the **tenant** has been in occupation for less than a year, a discretionary payment can be made. The level of payments are:

- 10% of the market value, with a minimum of £1,500 up to a maximum of £15,000, for **owner-occupiers**
- £1,500 in all other cases.

Occupiers may also qualify for a **disturbance payment**.

Home Release Scheme	Welsh equivalent of the **Tenants' Incentive Scheme**.
home repair assistance	Replacement for **minor works assistance** in the Housing Grants, Construction & Regeneration Act 1996.
Homebuy Option	A **low cost home-ownership** scheme administered by **Tai Cymru** which allows 70% ownership with a 30% rent-free holding held as a charge by the **housing association**.
homeless	The statutory definition of homeless in England & Wales relates to those who apply to a **local authority** for housing as a **homeless** household (or as being **threatened with homelessness**) and fulfil the statutory criteria set out in the **Housing Act 1996** of having:

1) no accommodation which they are entitled to occupy in the UK or elsewhere
2) accommodation but –
   - cannot secure entry to it
   - it is a moveable structure, vehicle or vessel and they have nowhere to place it where they are entitled to live in it
   - it is likely that occupation will lead to violence from another person living in it or threats of violence from someone likely to carry out the threats
   - it would be **unreasonable** for them to continue to occupy it
   - it is not available for the whole household, ie the applicant and any other person who normally lives with them and with whom it is **reasonable** to expect them to live.

The **local authority** only has statutory duty to provide housing to households **accepted as homeless** if they are:
- in **priority need**
- **eligible for assistance**
- **unintentionally homeless**
- and, there is no other suitable accommodation in the area.

At this stage, the authority will then consider whether the applicant has a **local connection** with any other authorities to which they may refer the applicant. If there is no **local connection** outside the area and all the other criteria are met, the authority must provide housing for the applicant. See **accepted as homeless (Scotland)**.

Homeless Families Initiative	**Housing Corporation** programme to target **ADP** resources towards the provision of housing for **homeless** families. The Corporation has a national target of a minimum of 50% of lettings in new developments for rent must be made available to the **homeless**, of which 60% must be **homeless**.
Homeless International	UK-based voluntary group which provides financial and technical support to **NGOs** and groups working to improve the shelter conditions of poor people in Europe, Asia, Africa, Latin America and the Caribbean. It supports the international exchange of information and experience of **homelessness** by facilitating links between organisations in the South and North.
Homes Above Retail Premises	Welsh equivalent of **Flats Over Shops**.
HOMES' Mobility Scheme	Initiative administered by **HOMES** to assist **local authority** and **housing association tenants** move home. This scheme can put **tenants** in touch with **housing associations**, **local authorities** and private **landlords**. Eligibility is restricted to those who:

- are taking up a job which is too far away to commute
- need to be closer to relatives or friends for support
- other pressing reasons such as domestic violence or **harassment**.

Closely allied to **Homeswap**.

homesteading	Schemes which allows **tenants** to purchase empty run down properties and undertake repair work. A discount may be given on the purchase price and the occupant may be eligible for grant aid from the **local authority**.

Homeswap Scheme	Initiative administered by **HOMES** to assist **local authority** and **housing association tenants** swap tenancies with other households wishing to move. Permission is needed from each **landlord**. Similar to the **HOMES' Mobility Scheme** but Homeswap does not cover private tenancies.
hostel	The statutory definition of a hostel in the **Housing Act 1985** is a building where accommodation is provided which is not self-contained and where either food or facilities for the preparation of food are provided. Many residents of hostels are **licensees**, but they may also be **tenants** depending on the kind of accommodation.
Hostel Deficit Grant	Discontinued grant, formerly available in England, to **special needs housing** schemes to cover the high running costs incurred by **hostel** facilities. Subsequently replaced by the **SNMA**.
House Builders' Federation	Trade federation for private sector builders in England & Wales.
house in multiple occupation	A building in which a number of separate households are resident under separate **tenancies** or **licenses**. Many different types of dwelling fall into the **HMO** category, including blocks of flats, houses divided into self-contained bedsits, **residential homes**, **shared housing**, lodgings, **hostels** and B&B hotels. The **Housing Act 1996** sets out a model for the introduction of a voluntary registration scheme for **HMOs** and provides new enforcement powers including higher penalties for transgression of registration and environmental health rules, planning restrictions on new **HMOs** in certain areas, a statutory duty of care placed on **landlords** and a requirement upon **local authorities** to ensure such properties provide adequate means of escape.
house renovation grants	Funding for **tenants** and **owner-occupiers** to improve and repair their homes, available through the **local authority**. Under the **Housing Grants, Construction & Regeneration Act 1996**, all English renovation grants become discretionary except **Disabled Facilities Grant**.
Housing	Official monthly magazine of the **Chartered Institute of Housing**.
Housing Act 1980	Introduced the **right to buy**, plus changes to the rights of **secure tenants**.
Housing Act 1985	Changed the rules governing **allocations, homeless** persons, the **right to buy**, house conditions and grants to deal with poor conditions. Also changed the rights and obligations upon **secure tenants**.
Housing (Scotland) Act 1987	Set out the statutory requirement of **local authorities** in Scotland to provide housing for **homeless** households, the rights conferred on **secure tenants**, the duties and powers surrounding dwellings which are **Below the Tolerable Standard** as well as the regulation of **HMOs** and **house renovation grants**.
Housing Act 1988	Set out current framework for **assured tenancies**, set up **Tai Cymru**, **Housing Action Trusts** and changed the **right to manage**.

Housing Act 1996	Attempts to unify access to **social housing** by changing the statutory **homeless** and **allocations** duties of **local authorities**. The duty to provide housing for households **accepted as homeless** is reduced to 24 months and an extra qualification of *'there being no suitable alternative accommodation in the area'* is added to the criteria for being **accepted as homeless**. The Act also expands the role of the **Housing Corporation** and **Tai Cymru** to incorporate the regulation and funding of **registered social landlords** (eg **local housing companies**). In turn, **HAG** will become **Social Housing Grant**. The **right to buy** is extended to **housing association tenants** through the **Statutory Purchase Grant** scheme and the **Housing Association Tenants Ombudsman Service** is put on a statutory footing. **Assured shorthold tenancies** become the default for all **tenancy agreements** and a framework for the development of **introductory tenancies** is put in place. A model voluntary **HMO** registration scheme is set out and new enforcement powers over **HMOs** are introduced. The **Tenants' Choice** scheme is also brought to an end.
Housing & Planning Act 1986	Introduced **Section 16 grants**.
Housing Action Area	An area of run-down housing which has been earmarked by the **local authority** for a package of measures to upgrade the stock and the environment through cash grants and direct provision. In England **HAAs** were superseded by **Renewal Areas** in the **Local Government & Housing Act 1989**, but they still continue in Scotland.
Housing Action Trust	Temporary body set up to repair and improve houses, encourage diversity of ownership and to improve living and social conditions and the general environment in run down areas of England and Wales. Currently, there are 6 **HATs**; Castle Vale, Liverpool, North Hull, Stonebridge, Tower Hamlets and Waltham Forest. A majority of **tenants** must vote in favour of the creation of a **HAT** before it can proceed. The **board of management** consists of **tenants** and **local authority** representatives as well as ministerial appointees. Land owned by the **HAT** and occupied by a **secure tenant** can only be disposed of to a **local authority** or to a **landlord** with **approved landlord status**. The **tenant** has the right to object to any disposal to any new **landlord** other than a **local authority**.
housing advice service	Organisation delivering advice about housing problems, provided by many **local authorities**. Additionally there is a network of independent housing advice agencies such as those run by **Shelter** which take on a greater advocacy role for their clients. The **Housing Act 1996** requires **local authorities** to ensure that advice and information about **homelessness** is available free of charge to everyone in their district.
housing association	Although there is no legal restriction on any organisation calling itself a housing association, for the purposes of this book and the vast majority of housing issues, the term housing association refers to a voluntary sector non-profit making organisation which provides, constructs, improves or manages or encourages/facilitates the provision of **social housing**. In general, housing associations provide homes for people on low income and in **housing need** and are registered with the **national housing agency**, but some only provide

services related to housing, these are known as **secondary housing associations**. Housing associations come in many forms, they may be **limited companies, trusts, charitable, Industrial and Provident Societies, co-operatives, almshouses, Abbeyfield Societies, registered** or non-**registered**. They may specialise in providing particular types of housing; temporary, special needs, supported, single people or families. Housing association **tenants** who became **tenants** after the 15 January 1989 (1/1/1989 in Scotland) have the same statutory rights as private sector **tenants** though they also have the benefit of the provisions in the **Tenants' Guarantee**. **Tenants** who became **tenants** of housing associations prior to the 15 January 1989 are **secure tenants**.

Housing Association Grant

Main public subsidy paid to **housing associations** by **central government**, through the **national housing agency** to finance new homes and **hostels** for rent, as well as **low cost home-ownership** schemes and the rehabilitation of properties. **HAG** is replaced by **Social Housing Grant** in the **Housing Act 1996**.

housing association liaison group

Forum for a **local authority** and **housing associations** to meet to discuss **social housing** issues and performance in the district.

housing association rules

The term used for the constitution of a **housing association** which is registered with the **Registrar of Friendly Societies** as an **Industrial and Provident Society**. The rules contain the **objects** of the association, its powers and the way in which it must conduct its business, eg the holding of meetings, voting etc. Changes to the rules must be registered with the **Registrar of Friendly Societies**.

Housing Association Tenants Ombudsman Service

Independent body, funded through the **Housing Corporation** providing a service to resolve complaints made against **registered housing associations**, to seek redress and help improve the quality of services provided. The **Housing Act 1996** places **HATOS** on a statutory footing independent of the **Housing Corporation** and able to investigate the actions of all **registered social landlords**. Similar bodies exist in Scotland & Wales, but are unaffected by the **Housing Act 1996**.

Housing Associations Act 1985

Covered the regulation of **housing associations, dualities of interest**, the financial framework for associations and the role of the **Housing Corporation**.

Housing Associations as Managing Agents

Scheme to encourage private **landlords** to transfer the management of their empty properties to **housing associations**, usually on a short-term basis. **Housing associations** then relet the properties to families receiving **Housing Benefit**. Unlike **HALS** arrangements, the **housing association** does not have a **contract** with the **tenant**, only the **landlord**.

Housing Associations Charitable Trust

A UK-wide grant making charity working to help voluntary organisations provide good quality housing and related services for:

- single **homeless** people with support needs
- older people
- refugee-led groups
- people with special needs
- black and minority ethnic communities.

HACT achieves these aims by:
- providing grants and loans
- giving fund-raising information and advice
- promoting housing issues to other charitable donors and assisting them in funding housing projects more effectively.

Housing Associations Leasing Scheme

Scheme under which **housing associations** lease properties from private sector owners and relet them to **tenants** in receipt of **Housing Benefit**. Unlike **HAMA** arrangements the **housing association** has a **contract** with both the **landlord** and the **tenant**.

Housing Associations Weekly

Former journal of the **National Federation of Housing Associations**, replaced with *Housing Today*.

housing authority

The housing functions of a **local authority**. Different authorities take on different responsibilities, some manage a large **housing stock**, others have no stock and only seek to meet their statutory duties towards the **homeless** and set out a strategic framework for housing provision in their area. Under **CCT** some authorities with stock have no day-to-day responsibility for housing management. Housing authority activities may stretch beyond the direct provision of homes to related services such as anti-crime programmes and accident prevention schemes etc.

Housing Benefit

Local authority administered, **means-tested** welfare benefit for low income households to contribute towards the cost of rented accommodation. The amount paid is based on rent, income, **Local Reference Rents** and an assessment of the household's housing requirements. The money may be paid to the **tenant** or direct to the landlord (**Rent Allowance**), but in the case of **local authority tenants**, it is paid in the form of **Rent Rebate**, which reduces the overall rent bill.

Housing Benefit cross-subsidy

The rent of **local authority tenants** who do not qualify for **Housing Benefit** is used to subsidise **Rent Rebate** for poorer **tenants** who do qualify.

Housing Benefit Direct

Housing Benefit payments paid directly to the **landlord** either at the request of the **tenant** or in cases where 8 or more weeks' **rent arrears** are owed.

housing bond

Proposed financial good which would allow the purchase of bonds whose value would be linked to the property market and would provide finance for housing projects.

Housing Centre Trust

Voluntary organisation working towards the provision of better housing by making representations to government and disseminating information on housing issues. The centre operates a library, publishes research, delivers seminars and runs a book shop specialising in housing literature. It is a membership organisation with members drawn from all areas of housing.

housing contractor unit

The **in-house team tendering** for a housing management **CCT** contract.

housing co-operative

See **co-operative housing association**.

Housing Corporation	The **national housing agency** for England. The Housing Corporation is a government agency sponsored by the **DoE** and was created by the Housing Act 1964 to register, fund, promote and supervise the **housing association** movement. Until 1989, it was responsible for the whole of Great Britain but now only has jurisdiction over England. **Tai Cymru** is its Welsh counterpart. **Scottish Homes** and the **Northern Ireland Housing Executive** perform many of the same functions with the addition of actually being **landlords**.
housing element of subsidy	The part of the subsidy from **central government** to **local authorities** to cover the general costs of running a housing service. The level of subsidy is calculated by comparing each authority's performance with its **management and maintenance allowances, guideline rent increases** and outstanding debts. Along with **Rent Rebate element of subsidy**, the housing element goes to make up **local authorities' HRA subsidy**.
Housing Finance Corporation (The)	An **I & P Society** set up through the **Housing Corporation** to attract long-term fixed-rate funding for **housing associations**. THFC raises a wide variety of loan finance for **social housing**, offers security to lenders and can acquire favourable rates for borrowers by forming **consortia** of **housing associations** seeking to raise finance.
Housing for Wales	See **Tai Cymru**.
housing gain (or loss)	The number of extra (or fewer) dwellings resulting from a re-**development** or refurbishment scheme.
Housing Grants, Construction & Regeneration Act 1996	Makes all **house renovation grants** discretionary apart from the **Disabled Facilities Grant**.
Housing Investment Programme (allocation)	**DoE credit approvals** to **local authorities** to meet the **capital** expenditure in their housing investment strategy. **HIP** allocations are made up of **ACG** and **SCG**. **Local authorities** bid each year to the **DoE** for their **credit approval**, part of which was, until 1996, determined by **GNI**. From 1997/8 all **HIP** allocations will be determined competitively at the local level.
Housing Investment Trust	An approved investment company to provide funds for the provision of private rented accommodation. **HITs** have preferential tax treatment under the **Finance Act 1996** to invest resources in **eligible residential properties**.
Housing Management Advisory Panel	A **Welsh Office** funded body which promoted good practice in housing management for **social housing landlords** in Wales. The panel was wound up in 1994.
Housing Management CCT	**Central government** policy requiring **local authorities** with housing operations above the **de minimis** threshold to put their housing management service out to **competitive tender**.
housing management plan	Plan which Scottish **local authorities** are required to prepare setting out their housing management policies including service delivery targets, **tenant** consultation arrangements and **tendering** procedures.

Housing Management Standards Manual

Chartered Institute of Housing publication setting down statutory obligations on housing providers and good practice for the efficient and effective disposal of their duties.

housing manager

Officer of a **local authority** or **housing association** responsible for the day-to-day management of the organisation's **housing stock**. Housing managers may become involved in a wide range of issues, from estate management to crime prevention.

Housing Market Package

Short-term programme of **Housing Corporation** funding in 1992/3 to assist **housing associations** buy empty properties on the open market. **Tai Cymru** ran a similar scheme known as the **Acquisitions Initiative**.

housing need

Loosely defined term to describe a lack of access to good quality housing at **affordable rents**, however many organisations use different concepts to describe housing need.

Housing Needs Index

Composite measure of **housing need** used by the **Housing Corporation** and **Tai Cymru** to calculate the need for **housing association** developments within a **local authority** area, although the Welsh version differs markedly from the English. The **HNI** is used, in part, to determine the regional distribution of the **ADP**.

housing needs survey

Survey to assess the extent and pattern of **housing need** in an area. There are many different methodologies employed for different types of survey, eg special needs, national needs, local needs. Many **local authorities** now carry out regular **housing needs** surveys in order to fulfil their responsibility for setting a strategic framework for the provision of housing in their area.

Housing Options Wales

Small grants awarded by the **Welsh Office** to organisations within Wales with the aim of promoting innovation and good practice in housing.

Housing Organisations Mobility and Exchange Services

A national agency funded by the government to work with **local authorities, housing associations** and **housing co-operatives** throughout the UK, to help people move home through the **HOMES'** **Mobility Scheme** or the **Homeswap Scheme**.

Housing Partnership Fund

A **challenge fund** administered by **IROs** on behalf of the **DoE** to promote innovative partnerships between **local authorities, central government**, other agencies and the private sector which are aimed at meeting **housing needs**.

Housing Plus

A concept which promotes the adoption of a society-wide perspective in the planning of new **housing association** developments. The issues may include employment, anti-crime strategies, accessing public services, healthy and sustainable environments and promoting community participation.

housing register

List of people seeking accommodation from a **local authority**. **Allocations** are made from the register.

Housing Repairs Account

Section of the **Housing Revenue Account** devoted to repairs and maintenance.

Housing Revenue Account	**Local authority** account for the running costs into which rents are paid. Money can be paid from this account to finance housing projects, service housing debts and cross-subsidise **Rent Rebates** to poorer **tenants**. This account is **ring-fenced** to prevent transfers of money from the authority's **General Fund**.
Housing Revenue Account subsidy	Money paid by **central government** to **local authorities** in England & Wales to cover any deficits in their notional **HRA**. The **HRA** subsidy is made up of the **Rent Rebate element** and the **housing element of subsidy**.
housing selection scheme	Mechanism used in Northern Ireland for administering the **housing register**.
housing society	Alternative name for a **housing association** usually associated with **Industrial and Provident Societies**.
housing stock	Term used to refer to all the dwellings under the ownership and management of a **landlord**.
Housing Support Grant	Payments to Scottish **local authorities** to cover estimated deficits on the **HRA**.
Housing Today	Successor to *HA Weekly*.
housing trust	A **housing association** required by its constitution or its **governing instrument** to use its funds to provide housing accommodation for charitable purposes. A housing **trust** may have a constitution which is a **trust deed** or it may be an **Industrial and Provident Society** or a **company limited by guarantee**.

I

I

I & P Society	See **Industrial and Provident Society**.
ICLEI	International Council for Local Environmental Initiatives
IEHO	See **Chartered Institute of Environmental Health**
IFS	Improvement For Sale
IOH	See **Chartered Institute of Housing**.
IRO	Integrated Regional Offices
IRRV	Institute of Revenues, Rating & Valuation
ISMI	Income Support for Mortgage Interest
implied surrender of tenancy	When a property is **abandoned** the **landlord** may proceed on the basis that the **tenant** has surrendered the **tenancy** and may **repossess** the property without a **court order**. Relevant factors in ascertaining whether there has been an implied surrender include whether the **tenant**: • is living permanently elsewhere • is claiming benefits from the address • has returned the keys to the **landlord** • has removed furniture and other belongings from the property • has visited the property in the recent past • has left anyone else living there. **Landlords** need to be careful about concluding that a **tenancy** has ended by implied surrender since if they are wrong, they may be guilty of illegal **eviction**. In Scotland **secure tenancies** are generally considered to have been surrendered if the **tenants** are absent from the house without **reasonable** cause for a continuous period exceeding 6 months.
Improvement For Sale	Scheme providing **HAG** for **housing associations** to purchase and modernise properties which are then sold at a market rate.
improvement grants	See **house renovation grants**.
imputed rent	The notional value which an **owner-occupier** receives from living in their home.
inadmissible items	Items which cannot be considered for subsidy, relief or grant, eg when applying for **HAG** a **housing association** cannot claim for the cost of providing garages, and nor can non-housing activities be considered for **Section 54 tax relief**. Also known as **non-qualifying costs** or **ineligible items**.
Incapacity Benefit	**Non-means tested, contributory, social security benefit** for people who are incapable of work through sickness or disability.
Income Support	A **non-contributory, means-tested social security benefit** for low income households without full-time work. It is aimed at meeting day-to-day living expenses (except rent).
Income Support for Mortgage Interest	That part of **Income Support** paid to **owner-occupiers**. The money goes towards meeting the interest payments on a **mortgage** and the amount is calculated on the basis of prevailing market rates.

indemnity insurance	Policy taken out by architects, surveyors etc. to insure against the costs of **liability** for defects arising from their work.
indenture	An old name for a **deed** between two or more parties, eg a **conveyance**, **lease** or **mortgage**.
Independent Living Fund	A state-funded charity which makes grants to assist applicants avoid institutional care.
index-linked	The principle of tying a series of payments to the **Retail Price Index**. The value of many items fluctuate according to changes in inflation, eg pensions and some **mortgages**.
indicator rents	Guideline rents issued to **housing associations** annually by the **NFHA**. Indicator rents are an approximation of what are considered to be **affordable rents**.
Industrial and Provident Society	An organisation registered under the Industrial & Provident Societies Act 1965 with the **Registrar of Friendly Societies**. Three quarters of **housing associations** are **I & P Societies**. To be eligible, the **housing association** must conduct its business for the benefit of the community or be a bona-fide **co-operative housing association**.
industrial housing association	A **housing association** originally set up to meet the **housing needs** of employees of a particular industry or company, eg Airways Housing Society.
ineligible items	See **inadmissible items**.
infill scheme	**Development** of a parcel of land located between existing buildings.
in-house team	**Contractor** made up from council team (eg **HCU** or **DSO**).
injunction	A **court order** requiring an individual to follow a prescribed course of action. They can be either: • mandatory – requiring certain action to be taken, eg to require a **landlord** to carry out repairs, or • prohibitory – requiring an individual to refrain from acts of **trespass**, damage to property etc. or a **tenant** not to breach the terms of the **tenancy**. Injunctions are increasingly favoured by **landlords** tackling **anti-social behaviour** because: • they can be obtained more quickly than **possession orders** • the defendant has little scope to delay proceedings • the burden of proof is less than for a criminal case • witnesses do not have to attend court for an **interim injunction** reducing the risk of witness intimidation. If an injunction is broken, the party that obtained it can take action for contempt of court which can lead to a fine or imprisonment. In Scotland, they are known as **interdicts**.
Innovation & Good Practice Grants	A programme of grants from the **Housing Corporation,** to finance **revenue expenditure** in **housing association** projects which deliver innovation and/or good practice in housing management. Successful projects must address current **Housing Corporation** themes and contain proposals for dissemination of information about the project to others.

input	Specified requirement in a **contract** such as office opening hours or number of staff on duty.
Inside Housing	Weekly magazine of the housing profession.
Institute of Housing	See **Chartered Institute of Housing**.
Institute of Independent Arbitrators	Professional body of arbitrators.
Institute of Revenues, Rating & Valuation	Professional body for people employed in **Housing Benefit** and **Council Tax** administration, local taxation and valuation rating. The **IRRV** promotes good practice, administers professional qualifications and advises **central government** and other bodies on pertinent legislative changes and related matters.
Institution of Environmental Health Officers	See **Chartered Institute of Environmental Health**.
Integrated Regional Offices	See **Government Offices for the Regions**.
intentionally homeless	See **unintentionally homeless**.
interdict	Scottish equivalent of an **injunction**. The major difference being that interdicts can only be negative (or prohibitory), ie require the person to cease.
interim injunction	An **injunction** which can be obtained as a temporary measure in court proceedings as an emergency remedy to prevent further loss or damage to one of the parties or to retain the status quo until the case reaches a final decision in the court. An interim injunction is issued to last for a fixed period of time or until the final hearing of the court action takes place. Interim injunctions are a useful tool in court action to deal with **anti-social behaviour** as they can be obtained quickly and require a low level of proof. Also called an **interlocutory injunction**.
interlocutory injunction	See **interim injunction**.
internal audit	An **audit** carried out to satisfy the internal requirements of an organisation. It is usual for this to be followed by an **external audit**.
International Council for Local Environmental Initiatives	Non-governmental body which promotes ecologically sensitive local development.
introductory tenancies	A new form of **tenancy** for England & Wales which can be used by **local authorities** and **HATs** limited to a **tenant's** first year of residence. **Landlords** have discretion whether to introduce an introductory tenancy scheme. If no court action for **repossession** has begun against the **tenant** when a year has expired, the **tenancy**

becomes a **secure tenancy**. Introductory tenancies are introduced in the **Housing Act 1996** and are primarily intended to tackle **anti-social behaviour**. They were previously known as **probationary tenancies**.

Invalid Care Allowance	A **non-means tested, non-contributory social security benefit** paid to the carer of a disabled person who gets **Attendance Allowance** or **DLA**.
ish	The date on which contractual **tenancy** ends, used in Scotland.
island council	Type of **unitary authority** in Scotland. Only three exist, Orkney, Shetland and Western Islands and they were unaffected by the **Local Government Review**.

JAWS	Joint Application Waiting List
JCT	Joint Contracts Tribunal
JRF	Joseph Rowntree Foundation
JSA	Job Seeker's Allowance

Job Seeker's Allowance
A hybrid **social security benefit** to replace **Income Support** for the unemployed and **Unemployment Benefit** from October 1996.

Joint Application Waiting List
A standard specification developed by the **NFHA** of information to be collected and used as a basis for **allocations** by partners in a **common housing register** scheme.

Joint Contracts Tribunal
Organisation which lays down and promotes the use of standard forms of building **contract**, including duties and responsibilities of all parties and default scenarios.

joint tenancy
A **tenancy** which is jointly held by two or more persons, eg husband and wife. When a joint **tenant** dies, the surviving **tenant**(s) can continue to rent the property even if they do not qualify for **succession**.

Joseph Rowntree Foundation
Independent, non-political charity which funds a programme of research and innovative development in the fields of housing, social care and social policy. Founded by Joseph Rowntree, who was perhaps more famous, as a confectioner!

judgment
A final decision by a court in any court action which can then be enforced. Judgments include **possession orders** and **injunctions**. Judgments also include **court orders** for the payment of debts such as **former tenants' arrears**.

junior minister
Central government minister without cabinet status. Most junior ministers report to a **Secretary of State** (only the Ministry for Agriculture, Fisheries and Food, the Treasury and the Lord Chancellor's Department do not have a **Secretary of State**). Junior ministers may be **Ministers of State** or **Under Secretaries of State**.

LA	local authority
LAHAG	**Local Authority Housing Association Grant**
LBA	**London Boroughs Association**
LCHO	**low cost home-ownership**
LEC	**Local Enterprise Company**
LGA	**Local Government Association**
LGIU	**Local Government Information Unit**
LGMB	**Local Government Management Board**
LHC	**local housing company**
LIBOR	**London Inter Bank Offered Rate**
LOTS	**Living Over The Shop**
LPAC	**London Planning Advisory Committee**
LRC	**London Research Centre**
LSVT	**Large Scale Voluntary Transfer**
Land Authority for Wales	Government body with responsibility for acquiring and disposing of land for **development** in Wales.
land bank	Parcels of land held for future **development**.
Land Register	See **HM Land Registry**.
landlord	Generic term for a provider of rented housing. Throughout this book the term **landlord** is used to refer to **local authorities (housing authority)**, **housing associations** and **private rented sector landlords**.
Large Scale Voluntary Transfer	Process by which all, or a substantial part, of a **local authority's housing stock** is **transferred** to another body, normally a **housing association** created especially for the purpose. The **transfer** is financed by a loan from a bank or **building society**, which enables **catch-up repairs** to be carried out on the properties. In many cases the authority also receives a substantial **capital receipt**. A ballot of **tenants** must take place before the **transfer** and approval from the **Secretary of State** is also needed.
latent defects	Construction defects which were not apparent at the time of completion.
lease	The grant of permission to occupy property with **exclusive possession** on certain conditions, usually including the payment of rent. Permission is given by a person who is entitled to possession of the property (the **landlord** or **lessor**). In some cases, the **landlord** will own the **freehold**. In other cases, the **landlord** may also be a **lessee**

under another lease in which case the lease to the **landlord** is known as the **head-lease** and the lease granted by the **landlord** is known as a **sub-lease**. A lease may be for a fixed period (eg one year) or for a period which continues indefinitely until notice is given to bring it to an end (eg a weekly or yearly lease which automatically continues until brought to an end by notice). Leases for periods exceeding three years must be granted using a **deed**. The term **lease** is interchangeable with the term **tenancy** but the word **lease** tends to be used for formal **deeds** between commercial organisations or for long-term arrangements, eg the grant of a 99 year lease of a flat. The term **tenancy** tends to be used for shorter-term arrangements where a **deed** is not used, eg a weekly **tenancy** granted by a **local authority** or a **housing association**.

leasehold	The housing **tenure** of a person who holds a **lease**. Although it could be used to describe most **tenants** it is in practice used to describe the status of an **owner-occupier** who has bought a flat and holds a **lease** that was originally for a lengthy period such as 99 or 125 years. **Leaseholders** usually pay a capital sum (known as a premium) when they buy their **lease** and then pay a small **ground rent**. They often have to pay **service charges** to their **landlord** who usually owns the **freehold**.
Leasehold Reform, Housing and Urban Development Act 1993	Introduced new rights for **leaseholders** to collectively acquire the **freehold** on their homes. And, introduced the **Rent to Mortgage** scheme for **secure tenants**. The Act also paved the way for the introduction of **HMCCT** by removing **secure tenants'** right of veto over changes to the management of their homes and launched the **management code** for housing. The **right to repair** and **right to compensation for improvements** were introduced in Scotland as well as **housing management plans**.
leaseholder	See **lessee**.
lender	See **mortgagee**.
lessee	The **tenant** in a **leasehold** arrangement. Also known as the **leaseholder**.
lessor	The **landlord** in a **leasehold** arrangement. Also known as the **freeholder**.
leverage	This term is used in a variety of contexts. In accountancy it refers to an organisation's ratio of debt to **equity**, but in other arenas it refers to the ratio of public to private money. Also known as **gearing**.
liability	Accounting term for financial obligations, ie debts.
licence	Permission to occupy a dwelling given to someone who is not a **tenant** or **owner-occupier**. By being granted a **licence** the person is not a **trespasser**. Cohabitees and family members of **tenants** are licensees but the term is more often used to describe an agreement between a **landlord** and an occupier giving the occupier permission to occupy certain kinds of accommodation. The legal rights of licensees are usually less than those of **tenants** as licensees do not have **security of tenure** under statute and licences do not normally

grant the right to **exclusive possession**. Licences are normally associated with **lodgers** and with **shared housing** such as **hostels**.

lifetime homes	A design concept for residential dwellings which aims to provide homes flexible enough to meet the needs of all types of occupant over the whole of their lives.
limited company	See **company limited by guarantee** and **company limited by shares**.
liquidated and ascertained damages	Sums deducted by the **client** from money paid to a **contractor** for failure to fulfil obligations contained within a **contract**.
liquidity	A measure of an organisation's ability to find funds at short notice, ie its cash holdings relative to its total **assets** and/or **liabilities**.
listed building	A building of special historic or architectural importance, recognised by the **local authority** and the **Secretary of State** for the Environment, although the register of listed buildings is administered by the **Department of National Heritage**. Specific consent is required for the demolition, renovation or any change of use of a listed building.
Living Over The Shop	**JRF** funded project to promote the use of vacant space above shops in town centres. The project offers information and advice to **local authorities**, **housing associations**, and other property owners.
loan stock	A fixed interest **security**. Also known as a **bond**.
local authority	Democratic municipal entity charged with administering **local government** in a particular area, often referred to as councils. **District councils**, **borough councils**, **metropolitan boroughs**, **regional councils**, **county councils** and **island councils** are all forms of **local authority**.
local authority associations	Generic name for representative bodies of **local government** such as the **AMA**, **ADC**, **ACC** and **COSLA**.
Local Authority Housing Association Grant	**Housing Association Grant** payments which are initiated by a **local authority** but for which the cash is provided by the **Housing Corporation**. However, the spending still counts against the **local authority's credit approvals** or **capital receipts**. **LAHAG** is only available in England.
local connection	**Local authorities** have a statutory duty to provide housing to households **accepted as homeless** only if they are:

  • in **priority need**
  • **unintentionally homeless**
  • **eligible for assistance**
  • and, there is no other suitable accommodation in the area.

At this stage, the authority may then consider whether the applicant (or anyone they might **reasonably** be expected to live with) has a local connection, statutorily defined as a district in which the applicant:

  • is, or was, normally resident, with the exception of people serving in the armed forces and those detained under an **Act of Parliament** (eg prisoners)

- is employed
- has family links
- or, has other special circumstances connecting them with the area.

If the applicant has a local connection with another **local authority**, they may be referred to that other authority for re-housing. There cannot be a referral if the applicant or anyone who might **reasonably** be expected to live with the applicant runs a risk of domestic violence in that other authority.

local council	Generic term for organisations at the lowest tier of the **local government** structure in two tier areas. Examples include **parish councils**, **town councils** and **community councils**. They have very few legal powers and are responsible for maintaining local memorials, village halls, playing fields, camp-sites, allotments, car parks, cemeteries and the obstruction of rights of way etc.
Local Enterprise Company	Scottish equivalent of **Training and Enterprise Councils**.
local government	Throughout this book local government is used to refer to **borough councils, district councils, county councils, island councils, area boards, metropolitan authorities councils** etc. as opposed to **central government**.
Local Government & Housing Act 1989	Covers political restrictions on **local government** officers, the financial regime under which **local authorities** operate (including **credit approvals, capital receipts, revenue** and **capital expenditure,** the **HRA** etc.). **Renewal Areas** and the **mandatory renovation grant** system were also put in place.
Local Government Act 1988	Introduced **CCT**.
Local Government Act 1992	Set up the **Citizen's Charter** and instigated the **Local Government Review**.
Local Government Association	Unified body of **local authorities** in England & Wales. The **LGA** replaces the **ADC, ACC** and **AMA** on 1 April 1997.
Local Government Boundary Commission for Scotland	Independent advisory body set up by the government with responsibility for periodic reviews of electoral arrangements and administrative areas for **local government** in Scotland.
Local Government Boundary Commission for Wales	Independent advisory body set up by the government with responsibility for periodic reviews of electoral arrangements and administrative areas for **local government** in Wales.
Local Government Commission for England	An independent advisory body which took over from the Local Government Boundary Commission in July 1992 to review and make recommendations to **central government** on whether there should be changes to the structure of **local government**, the boundaries of individual **local government** areas and their electoral arrangements.

Local Government Information Unit	A membership organisation of **local authorities** and trade unions. **LGIU** advises **local authorities** and local councillors on all aspects of government and public relations. Provides specialist analysis, advice and lobbying on current **local government** issues including finance and housing.
Local Government Management Board	Organisation which represents the interests of **local authorities**. The **LGMB** provides support and advice to **local authorities** across England & Wales. It commissions and conducts research and promotes good practice. Staff give guidance on a range of topics including management and personnel, staff development and negotiations over pay/conditions of service. **LGMB** also produces occupational standards on which **NVQ**s in housing are developed and holds the Secretariat of the Housing Sector Consortium.
Local Government Ombudsman	Independent statutory body with a duty to provide impartial investigation into complaints and injustice caused through mal-administration by **local authorities** and many of the activities of **New Towns, Urban Development Corporations, English Partnerships, Housing Action Trusts,** police and fire authorities, **local authority** joint boards, the National Rivers Authority and education appeal committees.
Local Government Review	Review of **local authority** structures set up in 1992 and conducted by the **Local Government Boundary Commission for Scotland,** the **Local Government Boundary Commission for Wales** and the **Local Government Commission for England.**
local housing company	A new form of **social housing** provider. **LHC**s have been suggested as organisations which could take over the **housing stock** owned by **local authorities** enabling private finance to be raised outside of the restrictions imposed on **local authority capital expenditure.** There are many **LHC** models currently under consideration each with different constitutional structures and varying degrees of **local authority** and **tenant** involvement. The **Housing Act 1996** will allow **local housing companies** to become **registered social landlords** and, like **housing associations,** they will then be able to compete for **Social Housing Grant** (formerly **Housing Association Grant**) as well as attracting **private finance** to renovate their stock. Provided they satisfy the requirements set out in the **Housing Act 1996,** they will be able to register with the **national housing agency.**
local housing corporation	A type of **local housing company,** which would be wholly owned by a **local authority.** Currently, the spending of such bodies is treated as **local authority** spending and counts against their **credit approvals (capital allocations** in Scotland). Changes to public borrowing rules would be necessary to free local housing corporations from such constraints.
local plan	A **development plan** which sets out the district's detailed planning policies and proposals for specific sites. Local plans are devised by non-**metropolitan authorities** and fit within the strategic framework set out in the **county council's structure plan.**
Local Reference Rent	A notional rent determined by a **rent officer** for assessing **private rented sector Housing Benefit** claims. The reference rent is the mid-

point of a range of **market rents** for similar **private rented sector** accommodation in the locality.

lodger

An individual living as part of the **landlord's** household. A lodger normally shares the facilities of the house but does not have the right of **exclusive possession** to occupy any of the rooms, ie they have a **licence**.

London Boroughs Association

Forum for London boroughs to discuss **local government** issues and to represent their views to **central government**. The **LBA** has now merged with the **Association of London Authorities** to form the **Association of London Government**.

London Boroughs Grant Scheme

Successor body to the **GLC** which approves and administers grants to voluntary organisations in London.

London Inter Bank Offered Rate

Rate of interest major banks charge each other in financial transactions, often used as a benchmark for loan rates.

London Planning Advisory Committee

Successor body to the **GLC** which co-ordinates cross-borough planning issues in London.

London Research Centre

Successor body to the **GLC** which finances research into the **local government** issues confronting London.

Lords Stages

In addition to the Commons Stages (**First Reading, Second Reading, Committee Stage, Report Stage** and **Third Reading**) of its passage through Parliament, a **Bill** is considered by the House of Lords and follows a broadly similar legislative process as that in the Commons. A **Bill** may be introduced in either House, but must eventually go through both Houses of Parliament.

low cost home-ownership

Generic term for initiatives which aim to extend home ownership to low income households, eg **DIYSO** and **TIS**.

LSVT association

A **housing association** set up to receive the stock of a **local authority** following **LSVT**.

LSVT levy

Money paid to the **Treasury** by some **local authorities** as part of a **stock transfer** to cover anticipated increases in **Housing Benefit**. Following the transfer, rents are expected to rise, generating extra demand for **Housing Benefit**. The sum is calculated as a percentage of the **local authority's capital receipt**. Only those authorities which obtain a net receipt from a transfer are liable.

MBC	metropolitan borough council
MEP	Member of the European Parliament
MIRAS	Mortgage Interest Relief At Source
MITR	Mortgage Interest Tax Relief
MoD	Ministry of Defence
MRP	minimum revenue provision
MSCA	most satisfactory course of action

maintenance allowance

The amount of expenditure, which it is assumed, a **landlord** needs to spend on **day-to-day repairs** and **planned maintenance** in order to provide a standard level of service. The **DoE** assesses each **local authority's** requirement and the **national housing agencies** do the same for each **housing association**. The **landlord's** entitlement to subsidy is then calculated using these figures.

maintenance contracts

A legal **contract** agreeing the responsibilities of a **contractor** undertaking maintenance duties on behalf of a **landlord**.

major repairs

Improvements to **housing association** stock which may qualify for **HAG** (or **SHG**) and are too large to be considered as part of their **maintenance** and **management allowance**. Major repairs do not qualify for **HAG** in Wales.

management agreement

Contract between a **landlord** and a **managing agent** to provide housing management services for a period of time, to an agreed level of quality and for an agreed price, eg a **CCT** or **TMO contract**.

management allowance

The amount of expenditure, which it is assumed, a **landlord** needs to spend on housing management functions in order to provide a standard level of service. The **DoE** assesses each **local authority's** requirement and the **national housing agencies** do the same for each **housing association**. The **landlord's** entitlement to subsidy is then calculated using these figures.

management code

1) A code of good housing management practice approved by the **Secretary of State** under the **Leasehold Reform, Housing and Urban Development Act 1993**. The code has no legal force but can be quoted in court proceedings to illustrate appropriate standards.

2) A statutory code for the management of **houses in multiple occupation** contained in **Statutory Instruments** issued by the **Secretary of State** under the **Housing Act 1985**. A **landlord** or manager who fails to comply with this code commits a criminal offence.

management committee

See **board of management**.

management void

A short-term **void** for which a prospective **tenant** has been earmarked, but has not yet been able to take up occupation. In general, it is accepted that most **local authorities** and **housing**

associations will need to have a **void** rate of around 2% for management purposes.

managing agent

Organisation (other than the **landlord**) appointed to be responsible for the management of a stock of dwellings. The use of managing agents has been promoted through initiatives such as **CCT** and **HAMA**.

mandatory renovation grant

A **means tested** grant paid under the **Local Government & Housing Act 1989** and made to owners of properties which are **Unfit for Human Habitation**, as well as those upon which statutory notices have been served. Under the **Housing Grants, Construction & Regeneration Act 1996**, all renovation grants except the **Disabled Facilities Grant** become discretionary.

marginal unit cost

Extra cost of an additional unit of work.

market rent

Theoretical concept to describe a rent which has been freely determined by the forces of supply and demand. **Private rented sector** rents are the closest real life approximation.

maturity

Point in time at which a loan or **bond** is repaid.

means tested

A welfare benefit to which entitlement and pay-outs are restricted by the claimant's financial resources.

mediation

Procedure for settling disputes between two parties. A mediator brings the two sides together and attempts to generate some agreement. Unlike **arbitration**, an agreement is not imposed on the parties. Mediation is being increasingly used to settle neighbour disputes.

member

A term with a number of uses.
1) **Local authority** councillors are often referred to as members.
2) In a **housing association** or a **company limited by shares**, a member is an individual who has a shareholding. As **housing associations** are **non-profit-making landlords** their members do not receive a dividend, only pay a nominal amount (usually £1) for their share and can only hold one share each. In **companies limited by shares** members may hold many thousands of shares and usually receive a dividend. In a **company limited by guarantee**, members undertake to pay a nominal amount (usually £1) if the company becomes insolvent but do not hold shares. Membership entitles an individual to attend and vote at the **AGM** and usually to take part in electing the **board of management** or directors.

Member of the European Parliament

Person elected to sit in the **European Parliament**. The UK has 87 of the Parliament's 518 **MEPs** (England 71; Scotland 8; Wales 5; voting in Northern Ireland is based on a system of proportional representation, one constituency covers the whole province, from which 3 members are elected).

merchant bank

An institution which supplies financial goods and services, eg loans and **securities**, unit trust management, foreign exchange dealing. Unlike high street banks, they do not provide personal banking services such as cheque accounts.

mesne profits	Money paid by illegal occupants of buildings or land to the person entitled to **possession** as compensation for the use and occupation of the property. In Scotland they are known as **violent profits**.
messengers at arms	Scottish **bailiff** for the Court of Session.
metropolitan authority	A **local government** entity in a metropolitan area. Nearly all large urban conurbations are designated metropolitan status. **Local authorities** in such areas are **unitary** and known as a **metropolitan borough council**.
metropolitan borough council	**Local authority** in a metropolitan area. They all have **unitary** status and so have responsibility for all **local government** activities within their area.
mid-landlord	Term used in Scotland for a **tenant** who is **sub-letting** their home.
Migrant Funds	A European Union programme which aims to: • encourage free movement within the **EU** • ensure rights to **social security benefits**, health and social services • ensure access to education, rights to housing and guarantee political rights. In the past, much of the money has gone to voluntary organisations, especially those involved with housing projects, eg **housing associations**. There are no published funding criteria, no list of projects funded, nor any monitoring procedure. Application forms are available from the **NFHA**.
MIND	Charity established to provide information and advice about the issue of mental health. Operates through a federated structure.
Mini-HAG	**Housing Association Grant** paid on specific projects which attempt to bring empty properties into use for a short period of time.
minimum revenue provision	Minimum payments which must be made from the **Housing Revenue Account** of English & Welsh **local authorities** toward repayment of debt. Also known as **provision for credit liabilities**.
Minister for Local Government, Housing & Urban Regeneration	**Junior minister** in the **DoE** with responsibility for housing. The titles and responsibilities of **junior ministers** (and occasionally **Secretaries of State**) are frequently changed.
Minister of State	See **junior minister**.
Ministry of Defence	**Central government** department with responsibility for the armed forces and defence procurement. The **MoD** is also one of the country's largest **landlords**.
minor works assistance	A generic term for a discretionary **means tested** benefit to cover the cost of small improvements to a private property. Minor works assistance is replaced by **home repair assistance** in the **Housing Grants, Construction & Regeneration Act 1996**.
minority protection agreement	A **contract** between **members** of a company which ensures a veto for minority views over certain issues. It is envisaged that **local housing companies** may have some form of minority protection agreement

giving the **local authority** a veto on certain issues as a safeguard against the potential loss of democratic **accountability**. Also known as a **golden share**.

mission statement

Statement outlining the core values, goals and objectives of an organisation.

mixed funding

Finance which has come from a number of sources. Many housing investment projects are now financed by mixed funding, usually a combination of public money such as **HAG** and private borrowing.

mixed use development

A **development** project which contains a range of different potential uses, such as residential properties and commercial properties.

mobility housing

Ordinary homes, not designed with special features for disabled occupants, but owing to their design are suitable for people with mobility problems. Mobility housing is most suitable for people who can manage around the home without a wheelchair, but may need a walking frame. **Wheelchair housing** is more suitable for people who are wheelchair dependent. Mobility housing must incorporate:
- ramped entrances and **flush thresholds**
- minimum width doorways of 0.775m and corridors of 0.9m
- bathroom and toilet at entrance level
- staircases capable of taking a stairlift, if the bedroom is located on the first floor.

model rules

Standard approved rules for **housing associations** seeking **registration** set down by the NFHA.

modular repair programmes

Management strategy which allows **tenants** to choose from a series of repair packages each providing a different level of service in exchange for an agreed rent increase.

mortgage

A financial loan secured on a piece of land or building giving the person who made the loan the right to gain **repossession** of the property and to sell it to repay the loan should the mortgagor default on repayment.

Mortgage Interest Relief At Source

Tax relief on **mortgage** interest payments which is given to the tax-payer at the time they make the **mortgage** payment, ie at source rather than being claimed back later from the Inland Revenue. It has the result of reducing the amount payable by the tax-payer for each instalment of interest.

Mortgage Interest Tax Relief

Tax deduction on mortgage interest payments.

mortgage protection insurance

An insurance policy taken out by a **mortgagor** to cover the cost of **mortgage** payments in the event of death, loss of income etc.

mortgagee

The creditor or **lender** in a **mortgage** arrangement, ie the bank or **building society**.

mortgagor

The debtor or borrower in a **mortgage** arrangement, eg an **owner-occupier** or a **housing association** which has taken out a **mortgage** loan.

most satisfactory course of action

On identifying an individual, or group of privately owned **unfit dwellings**, **local authorities** have a duty to consider what is the most satisfactory course of action to deal with them. The options are to serve a notice for repair, to declare a **clearance area** or to serve a **closure notice** on the property's owner. The **Housing Grants, Construction & Regeneration Act 1996** introduces a further option; to defer action.

move-on accommodation

Permanent housing for people moving out of institutional care or **supported housing** to take up a more independent lifestyle.

Move-On Grant

Money from the **Housing Corporation** available to **registered housing associations** for the provision of **move-on accommodation** for people leaving institutional care under the **Care in the Community** programme.

multi-occupied

Building containing more than one household, eg **HMO**.

multiple contract authorities

Those authorities which have divided their housing management functions into more than one **service contract**.

mutual exchange

Swap of homes between two **tenants**. Schemes such as **Homeswap** and **HOMES' Mobility Scheme** allow longer distance moves. **Secure tenants** and **assured tenants** are entitled to exchange with their **landlord's** consent, which can only be withheld on certain specified statutory grounds.

NACAB	National Association of Citizens' Advice Bureaux
NACRO	National Association for the Care and Resettlement of Offenders
NAO	National Audit Office
NATWHAG	National Wheelchair Action Group
NCOPF	National Council for One Parent Families
NCVO	National Council of Voluntary Organisations
NDPB	non-departmental public body
NEA	National Energy Action
NFHA	National Federation of Housing Associations
NGO	Non-Governmental Organisation
NHBC	National House Builders' Council
NHER	National Home Energy Rating
NHF	National Housing Federation
NHF	National Housing Forum
NHTPC	National Housing & Town Planning Council
NIFHA	Northern Ireland Federation of Housing Associations
NIHE	Northern Ireland Housing Executive
NJCC	National Joint Consultative Committee for Building
NNDR	National Non-Domestic Rate
NOSP	notice of seeking possession
NRA	Neighbourhood Renewal Assessment
NTO	National Tenants' Organisation
NTRF	National Tenants' & Residents' Federation
NVQ	National Vocational Qualification
National and Scottish Vocational Qualification	Introduced in 1993, **NVQs** (and SVQs) are a nationally recognised qualification geared towards studying whilst in employment. **NVQs** in housing are competence based and modularised so that they can be studied when circumstances allow and have no specific entry requirements.
National Association for the Care and Resettlement of Offenders	Charitable organisation working with ex-offenders.

National Association of Almshouses	Representative body of **Almshouse Trusts**.
National Association of Citizens' Advice Bureaux	National umbrella organisation of **CABx**, providing support, training and guidance to local **CABx** as well as lobbying government for its clients' interests.
National Association of Local Councils	The representative body for **town**, **parish** and **community councils** in England & Wales. It provides legal, financial and general advice as well as a policy unit to represent members' interests.
National Audit Office	External **audit** body for **central government**, headed by the **Comptroller & Auditor General**. The **NAO** provides independent information, assurance and advice to Parliament and the public about all aspects of the financial operations of **central government**. The **NAO** is financed by Parliament and reports to the **Public Accounts Committee**.
National Council for One Parent Families	Pressure group working for the prosperity and independence of lone parents in England & Wales. **NCOPF** publishes advice for lone parents and professionals working to meet their needs, undertakes research and lobbies government on relevant issues.
National Council of Voluntary Organisations	Representative body of voluntary sector organisations. **NCVO** provides advice and support to local voluntary organisations and promotes its members' interests. The Scottish Council for Voluntary Organisations performs this role in Scotland.
National Energy Foundation	Charitable organisation which manages a network of local energy advice centres and is closely linked with **National Energy Services Ltd.** which administers the **National Home Energy Rating**.
National Energy Services Ltd.	A sister organisation of the **National Energy Foundation** which oversees the **National Home Energy Rating** and provides technical advice and training on energy efficiency issues.
National Federation of Housing Associations	Former name of the representative body of **housing associations** in England. The **NFHA** has now changed its name to the **National Housing Federation** to reflect changes in its membership following the **Housing Act 1996**.
National Home Energy Rating	Counterpart home energy rating scheme to **Starpoint** administered by the **National Energy Foundation**. It measures the **energy efficiency** of a house on a scale of 0 (very inefficient) - 10 (very efficient). A building's thermal performance is based on criteria including orientation, location, height above sea level, size, fuel type, heating and hot water system as well as household appliances. See **Standard Assessment Procedure (SAP)**.
National House Builders' Council	A private non-profit distributing company which sets construction standards for almost all new homes in the UK, acts as a regulator over registered house builders and provides a range of warranty and technical services to the house building industry and its customers.
national housing agency	Term used throughout this book to refer to the major **non-departmental public body** in each county of the UK with

responsibility for **social housing**, ie **the Housing Corporation, Scottish Homes, Tai Cymru** and the **Northern Ireland Housing Executive**. Each performs a different set of functions but none perform all the roles traditionally associated with a national housing agency.

National Housing & Town Planning Council

Independent organisation acting as a forum for **local authorities, housing associations**, house builders, developers, individuals and all those involved in **social housing** and planning in the public and private sectors. It campaigns for better housing and planning policies, promotes better practice, organises conferences and seminars and produces publications.

National Housing Federation

The new name for the **National Federation of Housing Associations** to reflect its broader membership following the introduction of **local housing companies** in the **Housing Act 1996**. The **NHF** seeks to spread ideas and information among its members, to provide services and to represent **registered social landlords'** views to government, **local authorities** and other bodies. It also publishes *Housing Today*, undertaking research and training activities and compiles **CORE** statistics.

National Housing Forum

An alliance of housing organisations in England & Wales. **NHF** lobbies on housing issues and organises National Housing Week which takes place annually in early June and is a week of events and campaigning to attract publicity for housing issues. Its members include the **ACC, ADC, Age Concern, AMA, CHAS, CIEH, CIH, Housing Centre Trust, NFHA, NHBC, NHTPC, RICS, RIBA, RTPI, Shelter** and **TPAS**.

National Joint Consultative Committee for Building

Industry funded body which sets down good practice for construction industry **contracts**.

National Loan Fund

Central government fund from which money is paid to the **Housing Corporation** and other public bodies.

National Non-Domestic Rate

An annually fixed rate, set by **central government** and used to calculate the **local government** tax to be levied on non-domestic properties. The **rateable value** of the property is multiplied by the **NNDR** to find the final amount.

National Tenants' & Residents' Federation

Umbrella body for **tenants'** and residents' federations in England. It works closely with **NTO** and **TPAS** with whom it has developed a **Tenant Participation** Charter.

National Tenants' Organisation

Umbrella body for tenants' **associations** in England. It works closely with **NTRF** and **TPAS** with whom it has developed a **Tenant Participation** Charter.

need group

Collective name for a group of applicants for **social housing** into groups such as **transfers, homeless** households etc.

negative equity

Phenomenon where the current market value of a property is lower than the outstanding **mortgage** for which it provides **security**.

Neighbourhood Energy Action	Charity seeking to alleviate **fuel poverty** through practical action and policy development. **NEA** is also the lead body for the **NVQ** in Domestic Energy Efficiency.
neighbourhood nuisance	See **nuisance**.
Neighbourhood Renewal Assessment	An assessment of an area's suitability for **Renewal Area** status. The study should consider social and economic issues as well as the quality of the housing.
Neighbourhood Watch	A police sponsored scheme in which residents agree to notify the police of any unusual happenings in their area.
net present value	Using **discounted cash flow** methods, the value of income and expenditure over time is given by the net present value. This approach factors in the **opportunity cost** of not putting the money in a secure account where it could have earned interest.
net worth	The value of an organisation. Calculated by subtracting the organisation's **liabilities** from current and fixed **assets**.
New Life for Urban Scotland	Scottish equivalent of **Estate Action**.
New Town	Direct descendent of **Garden Cities** which came to the fore after World War II. New Towns took advantage of cheap land on **green field sites** to develop mixed communities in social housing. It is estimated that three-quarters of a million homes were provided by New Towns during the post-war period. Examples include Warrington, Milton Keynes and Harlow.
NHS and Community Care Act 1990	Introduced the policy of **Care in the Community**.
nominal interest rate	The simple rate of interest without any adjustments, as opposed to real interest rates which are interest rates adjusted for inflation and expressed in **real terms**.
nomination agreement	A formal arrangement whereby households are allocated **housing association** or **private rented sector** accommodation as a result of an arrangement between the **local authority** and the **landlord**. Many **local authorities** have formal arrangements with local **housing associations** which allow them to have nomination rights over an agreed percentage of an association's properties.
non-charitable housing association	A **housing association** which does not have charitable status, allowing it to carry out a wider range of activities than a **charitable housing association**, eg it can build houses for sale. A non-charitable housing association can register with the **national housing agency** provided it is registered as an **Industrial and Provident Society**, and is a **non-profit-making landlord**. **Secure tenants** of non-charitable housing associations have the **right to buy**.
non-commercial considerations	Matters which authorities cannot consider when letting **CCT contracts**, eg the **in-house** or local team cannot be favoured except for commercial reasons.

non-contributory	Term used to describe **social security benefits** which can be claimed without having made National Insurance payments, eg **Income Support** and **Attendance Allowance**.
non-departmental public body	See **quango**.
non-dependent	A member of a household who it is assumed is financially independent from the benefit claimant, eg children over the age of 18 living with their parents. For **Housing Benefit**, non-dependents are assumed to make a financial contribution towards the claimant's housing costs, thus reducing the benefit pay out.
non-HRA	Term used to describe **local authority** housing expenditure which does not come out of the **Housing Revenue Account**. This money is generally used to finance private sector renewal programmes.
non-means tested	A welfare benefit to which everyone is entitled, regardless of their wealth. The amount of money received is also not affected by the claimant's financial resources, eg **Child Benefit**.
non-profit-making landlords	General term for a non-statutory organisation providing **social housing** at **affordable rent** levels, this includes **housing associations** and **local housing companies**.
non-qualifying costs	See **inadmissible items**.
Northern Ireland Federation of Housing Associations	Representative body of **housing association**s in Northern Ireland, its sister bodies in Great Britain are the **NFHA**, **WFHA** and **SFHA**. The **NIFHA** also consults with the Irish Council for Social Housing on cross border projects.
Northern Ireland House Condition Survey	Northern Irish equivalent of the **English House Condition Survey**.
Northern Ireland Housing Council	Advisory body to the **Northern Ireland Housing Executive** made up of nominees from each of the Province's 26 **district councils**.
Northern Ireland Housing Executive	The **NIHE** is the largest **landlord** in the UK, managing a stock of over 148,000 homes which were transferred from all of the Province's **local authorities** in 1971. Its executive body comprises 3 nominees from the **Northern Ireland Housing Council** and 7 ministerial appointees. The **NIHE** manages and maintains its own stock, has the power to build new homes, provides grant aid to the private sector, examines housing conditions and requirements, devises a housing strategy for the Province and has statutory responsibility for housing the **homeless**.
Northern Ireland Housing Trust	Post-war housing authority to assist in the construction and management of public housing, mainly for employed people outside the Belfast county area. Dissolved with the formation of the **NIHE**.
notice of intention	Notice sent to the *Official Journal of European Communities* giving advance information about a **local authority's** intention to award a **contract** on a competitive basis and containing basic details of the proposed **contract**.

notice of intention to raise proceedings	Scottish equivalent of **notice of seeking possession** for **assured** and **short assured tenancies**.
notice of offer	Under the **right to buy**, the **landlord** must issue the prospective owner with a notice of offer which details the market value, discount selling price, terms of the **conveyance** and provides other information about the proposed sale. Also referred to as an **offer notice**.
notice of proceedings for recovery of possession	Scottish equivalent of **notice of seeking possession** for **secure tenancies**.
notice of seeking possession	The document which must be served on an **assured tenant** or a **secure tenant** by a **landlord** wanting to gain **repossession** of a property before court proceedings can begin.
notice to quit	A legal document from either **landlord** or **tenant** notifying the other of their intention to terminate a **periodic tenancy**. The conditions and procedures required for the notice to be legally valid vary from **tenancy** to **tenancy**.
nuisance	Behaviour that **unreasonably** interferes with other people's rights to the use and enjoyment of their home and community, such as playing loud music at night. There are 3 legal categories of nuisance: 1) there is a **tort** (or **delict**) of nuisance where the person affected by the nuisance can take legal action for compensation or an **injunction** 2) a **landlord** may have **grounds for possession** when a **tenant** or a person living with a **tenant** has committed a nuisance or annoyance to neighbours 3) a **local authority** or a person affected can take action where there has been a **statutory nuisance**.

OMVEU	Open Market Value for Existing Use
OPP	**Outline Planning Permission**
OPSS	**Office of Public Service & Science**
objects	The aims of an organisation set out in its constitution, eg a **registered social landlord** is only permitted to have certain objects relating to housing which are set out in the **Housing Act 1996**.
offer notice	See **notice of offer**.
Office of Public Service & Science	Section of the **Cabinet Office** with responsibility for the **Citizen's Charter**, among other things.
One Parent Benefit	A supplement to **Child Benefit** for lone parents.
opportunity costs	The value of an asset expressed in terms of the utility which could have been gained by using the resources which purchased the asset in another way. For example the opportunity cost of re-roofing a building could be double-glazing and an entry phone system.
Option Land Bank	Generally county-wide organisations funded primarily by the **Rural Development Commission** and **local authorities**. Their remit is to negotiate with landowners to secure options on sites which will be sold on to **housing associations** solely for the provision of housing at **affordable rents** in rural areas.
order for possession	See **possession order**.
Order in Council	A legislative instrument, frequently used in Northern Ireland for establishing policy without the need for parliamentary debate.
Our Future Homes	Government **White Paper** published in June 1995 as a precursor to the **Housing Act 1996**.
out of area placement	The **allocation** of accommodation to households **accepted as homeless** which is outside the **local authority** area. Authorities in London have an agreement system covering such placements.
outline planning permission	Preliminary planning permission given by a **local authority** to a developer or landowner for particular **development** on a specific site. This assists the developer in raising finance without incurring the costs of preparing the detailed plan required for full planning permission.
output specification	Describes results to be achieved by a **contractor**, expressed in terms of performance and quality standards.
out-turn costs	See **final account**.
overcrowded	Term with many different definitions but defined in law as **statutorily overcrowded**.
overpayment	Benefit paid out to which the recipient is not entitled, eg **Housing Benefit** after tenancy termination.
owner-occupier	An individual or household who owns and lives in their own home usually through a **mortgage**. The term can be applied to both **freeholders** and **leaseholders**.

PAC	Public Accounts Committee
PATH	Positive Action Training in Housing
PC Sum	See **prime cost sum**.
PCL	**provision for credit liabilities**
PEP	**Priority Estates Project**
PESC	**Public Expenditure Survey Committee**
PFI	**Private Finance Initiative**
PI	**performance indicators**
PIA	**Priority Investment Area**
PIPA	**Private Investment Priority Area**
PPG	**Planning Policy Guidance**
PRC	Pre-Reinforced Concrete
PRS	**private rented sector**
PSBR	**Public Sector Borrowing Requirement**
PSFD	**Public Sector Financial Deficit**

par value housing co-operative
A **co-operative housing association** in which each member holds a nominal £1 share. However, the shareholding does not accrue dividends, nor does it change in value over time and nor does it entitle the member to any claim over the **equity** of the co-operative.

parish council
See **local council**.

Parker Morris Standards
Design standard set in 1961 for residential dwellings. They were mandatory until 1981 but are still seen as a bench-mark for internal space and heating requirements in new housing developments. Examples are: heating facilities should be capable of generating temperatures of 65°F (18.5°C) in living areas and 55°F (13°C) in the kitchen and hallways; minimum floor space should be 910 sq ft plus 50 sq ft storage space for a five person house.

Parliamentary Under-Secretary of State for Housing
Minister in the **Scottish Office** with responsibility for housing.

Part III homes
Accommodation for people with special needs, originally defined in Part III of the National Assistance Act 1948. If they provide board and personal care they are now required to register under the Registered Homes Act 1984.

partial transfer
Process of a **local authority** transferring part of its stock to a **housing association** or **local housing company** rather than the whole stock as in **LSVT**.

past tenants' arrears	See **former tenants' arrears**.
pattern book	A manual of approved designs from **Tai Cymru** which recommends layouts for new **housing association** properties.
performance audit	The term for **regulatory review** used in Wales (and formerly in England).
performance indicators	Factors which are measured to produce an assessment of an organisation's performance. **PIs** covering housing management, finance and development performance are used by the **Housing Corporation** to assess the relative performance of **registered housing associations**.
performance standards	Standards established by **Tai Cymru** against which the performance of Welsh **housing associations** are assessed through **performance audit**.
periodic assured tenancy	Type of **tenancy** which **housing associations** enter into with their **tenants** but can also be used by **landlords** in the **private rented sector**. The **tenancy** cannot be brought to an end unless the **landlord** has **grounds for possession** and has obtained a **court order**.
periodic tenancy	A **tenancy** which runs indefinitely being continuously renewed for short periods, eg weekly or monthly, without the need for any new **tenancy agreement** to be signed. Periodic tenancies do not exist in Scotland, however tenancies can be regularly renewed through **tacit relocation**.
peripatetic warden	**Warden** service which covers a number of dispersed properties rather than a project or estate.
permissions to borrow	See **credit approvals**.
Personal Allowance	An element of the **Applicable Amount** which varies according to family size.
persons from abroad	A benefit claimant who fails one of the following tests: • **Habitual Residence Test** • Rights Of Residence Test (**EU** claimants) • Immigration Status Test (non-**EU** claimants). Persons from abroad are not entitled to **non-contributory** benefits but may qualify for some **contributory** benefit payments.
physical disability	A medical condition which affects an individual's functional ability.
planned maintenance	Repairs to **housing stock** which are foreseen and should be financed by money set aside for that purpose. Planned maintenance includes servicing and repairs to systems such as lifts and heating. Preventative works such as painting and large-scale works such as roof renewal are also categorised as planned maintenance. The large costs involved in planned maintenance are met from a variety of sources including rental income and reserves. Much planned maintenance can be classified as **cyclical maintenance**.

planning blight	Deterioration in the condition or reduction in the valuation of a piece of land which has occurred because of an expectation that the land or neighbouring land is to be **developed**, eg the building of a major new road near by.
planning gain	Legal agreements which **local authorities** enter into with developers in order to secure the provision of social facilities such as educational, recreational, sporting and other community facilities. Sometimes used to lever affordable housing into private developments, usually through **Section 106 agreements**. Requirements imposed on developments using **Section 106 agreements** are technically known as **planning obligations**.
Planning Guidance (Wales)	Unified planning guidance for Wales.
planning obligations	see **planning gain**.
Planning Policy Guidance	Guidance issued by the **Secretary of State** for the Environment detailing national planning policy within existing legislation. There are 24 **PPGs**, key examples include:

PPG 1 – General Policy & Principles
PPG 2 – Green Belts
PPG 3 – Housing
PPG 5 – Simplified Planning Zones
PPG 7 – Countryside & Rural Economy
PPG 12 – Development Plans & Regional Planning Guidance
PPG 13 – Transport
PPG 14 – Development On Unstable Land
PPG 15 – Historic Buildings & Conservation Areas
PPG 16 – Archaeology & Planning
PPG 18 – Enforcing Planning Control
PPG 24 – Planning & Noise.

points system	A prioritisation system based on points allotted to applicants according to their level of need. **Allocations** from the **housing register** for **local authority** housing are usually points based. Each applicant's score is determined by factors such as the number of children in the household, the inadequacies of their present housing, **overcrowding** and any special requirements such as those arising from disability and medical need.
Poll Tax	See **Community Charge**.
positive action	Concept which attempts to increase the proportion of minority or disadvantaged groups within an organisation and to ensure the services it provides meet the needs of all groups within the community.
Positive Action Training in Housing	Scheme to encourage members of black and ethnic minority communities to train for a career in housing. **PATH** also aims to create an awareness within housing organisations of the under-representation of black people in middle and senior management positions.
possession	See **repossession**.

possession order

A **court order** granting **possession** of a property entitling the **landlord** to request the court bailiff to **evict** the occupant. Also known as an **order for possession** or a **decree for possession** in Scotland.

poverty trap

A work dis-incentive arising out of the welfare benefits system whereby individuals receive very little extra income in work, than they would if they remained on benefits.

pre-emption rights/ terms

Option for a seller of a property to repurchase it if and when the new owner decides to sell it on. **Housing association tenants** who exercise the **right to buy** in certain rural areas must give first refusal to the association from whom they purchased it.

Premium

Part of the assessment of a claimant's entitlement to a **means tested** benefit. The Premium is added to a **Personal Allowance** to give the total **Applicable Amount**.

preservation order

A **local authority** decision that a building should not be altered or demolished. They are often used as a precursor to a building becoming **listed**. **Local authorities** can also make tree preservation orders prohibiting any cutting down or pruning of a tree without their consent.

pre-tenancy determinations

An assessment by a **rent officer** of the maximum rent which **Housing Benefit** would cover if a claim were made on that dwelling. Used to help a prospective **tenant**/claimant to determine whether they could afford to live in a particular property. The **Housing Act 1996** allows **landlords** to request pre-tenancy determinations from the **local authority** as well, but for a fee.

prime cost sum

Amount allowed for in a **development contract** to cover the cost of fixtures and fittings or other quantities which are difficult to specify beforehand.

principal

The initial debt taken on when a loan is arranged, excluding the future interest which will be incurred. Also known as the **capital sum**.

prior information notice

Notice sent to the *Official Journal of the European Communities* at the beginning of each financial year by a **local authority** providing details of **contracts** for which it expects to seek offers or **tenders** during the year.

Prior Options Study

First stage of a **Financial Management and Policy Review** which assesses whether the functions of the **quango** under review could be better managed by privatisation, contracting out or transferring all or part of its functions to another body.

Priority Estates Project

An independent, not for profit housing consultancy providing housing-related services to **social housing landlords**, residents' groups and other housing-related organisations. **PEPs** work covers a wide range of housing issues including: housing management, resident participation, estate improvement, independent advice to **tenants** on **stock transfers**, training, community development in regeneration schemes, multi-agency working, social surveys and research.

priority investment areas
Areas of poor housing provision designated by the regional offices of the **Housing Corporation**. These areas have a priority in the allocation of public funds.

priority need
Term used to assess **homeless** applicants' entitlement to housing. To be accepted for re-housing under the **Housing Act 1996** an applicant must be **homeless** (or **threatened with**), in priority need, **unintentionally homeless** and **eligible for assistance**. Applicants are in priority need if they:
- are pregnant, or live with or might **reasonably** be expected to live with someone who is pregnant
- have dependent children who live with them or might **reasonably** be expected to live with them
- are vulnerable as a result of old age, mental illness, mental handicap, or **physical disability**, or some other special reason, or live with such a person or might **reasonably** be expected to live with them
- are **homeless** or **threatened with homelessness** as a result of an emergency such as flood, fire or other similar disaster.

Local authorities in England & Wales have a duty to provide advice and assistance to applicants who are **homeless** or **threatened with homelessness** but not in priority need to help them obtain their own accommodation, whereas in Scotland the **local authority** has a duty to provide interim accommodation pending enquiries.

private finance
Money raised from non-governmental sources, eg banks and **building societies**. Since 1988, **housing associations** have had to supplement the **HAG** they receive from government with private finance.

Private Finance Initiative
A **central government** programme launched in Autumn 1992 to attract **private finance** and skills to public sector capital projects. **English Partnerships** and the **Single Regeneration Budget** are two of the biggest **PFI** type schemes with a housing element.

Private Investment Priority Area
An area of inner city Northern Ireland ear-marked for housing investment through the promotion of private sector capital.

private rented sector
Rented housing owned by private **landlords**, ie not a **local authority**, **housing association, Housing Action Trust, housing trust, local housing company, housing co-operative, New Town** Corporation, **Urban Development Corporation** or **central government** department.

Private Sector Leasing
Schemes under which **local authorities** take out leases on private sector properties and relet them to **homeless** families. A **housing association** is often appointed as a **managing agent** for the properties.

probationary tenancy
See **introductory tenancy**.

professional indemnity insurance
See **indemnity insurance**.

professional witness
A person who gives evidence in a legal case who is doing so as part of his or her job rather than because they live in the area. Professional witness schemes are increasingly being used when tackling **anti-**

social behaviour as **tenants** themselves often fear reprisals and intimidation. In such instances, the professional witness is likely to be a housing officer, police officer or a private investigator who has been employed to collect evidence.

progressive	Term used to describe a cost which hits wealthier households proportionately harder than poorer ones, eg Income Tax, which is progressive by virtue of the different tax bands. As opposed to **regressive** taxes such as **VAT** and the **Poll Tax**.
property revenue account	Section of a **housing association's** account which charts the income and expenditure arising from the occupation, management and maintenance of the stock.
Property Specific Rent	A **reasonable market rent** determined by a **rent officer** for that type of property in a **private rented sector Housing Benefit** claim. Used to determine the **Appropriate Rent**.
protected tenancy	Form of **tenancy** granted by **landlords** in the **private rented sector** prior to 15 January 1989. Protected **tenants** from that period retain that status as long as they remain with the same **landlord**. **Fair Rents** can be registered with the **rent officer** setting the maximum rent payable under a protected **tenancy**. A protected **tenant** has **security of tenure** and so can only be evicted where the **landlord** has **grounds for possession**.
provision for credit liabilities	Money which **local authorities** must **set-aside** to cover their debts from **capital receipts**. Also known as **minimum revenue provisions**.
Public Accounts Committee	House of Commons **Select Committee** with responsibility for reporting on the financial and management performance of **central government** departments, agencies and programmes. Works closely with the **National Audit Office** and the **Comptroller and Auditor General**.
public corporation	A corporate body producing marketable goods at economically significant charges, but which is controlled by and accountable to government, eg the Post Office.
Public Expenditure Survey Committee	**Central government** inter-departmental committee which co-ordinates public expenditure decision making.
Public Health (Scotland) Act 1987	Instituted **statutory nuisance** framework in Scotland.
public liability insurance	Indemnity policy which insures an organisation against claims from members of the public. All **housing associations** have such policies as do the vast majority of **local authorities**.
public sector	Broad description which includes both **general government** and **public corporations**.
Public Sector Borrowing Requirement	The annual balance between revenue and expenditure in **local government, central government, public corporations** and other public bodies. It is the primary measure of budgetary deficits used in the UK. Although it measures the **public sector's** need for finance

from other sectors, it excludes borrowing and includes privatisation receipts. Unlike **GGFD**, it is not an internationally recognised accounting convention.

Public Sector Financial Deficit

Measure of the balance between **public sector** spending and income as measured on an **accruals accounting** basis.

qualifying costs	Items which can be considered for subsidy, relief or grant, eg all those items a **housing association** can refer to in an application for **HAG**. The opposite of **inadmissible items**.
qualifying person	Someone who is eligible to go on to the **housing register**. Certain groups of people do not qualify for entry on to the register, such as **persons from abroad**.
qualifying tender	**Tender** from an external bidder which undercuts the **in-house** bid.
Quality In Town & Country	Discussion paper issued by the **Department of the Environment** on design issues.
quango	Quasi Autonomous Non-Governmental Organisation. Government body with devolved responsibility for carrying out **central government** duties. Quangos may be executive, ie have spending powers such as the **Housing Corporation** or merely advisory such as the **Social Security Advisory Committee**. Also known as **non-departmental public bodies**.
quiet enjoyment	An obligation automatically implied and imposed on the **landlord** in any **lease** or **tenancy**. It does not mean that the **tenant** will enjoy the premises quietly, ie without any noise or **nuisance** from others. It means that as long as the **tenancy** continues and the **tenant** pays the rent and complies with the **conditions of tenancy**, the **landlord** will not interfere with the **tenant's** enjoyment and use of the premises. For example, the **landlord** breaches this obligation if s/he illegally **evicts** the **tenant**, enters the premises without permission or disconnects the water supply without good reason.

RAC	rent assessment committee
RCCO	**Revenue Contributions to Capital Outlay**
RDA	**Redevelopment Area**
RDC	**Rural Development Commission**
RDG	**Revenue Deficit Grant**
RFC	**Rate Fund Contribution**
RHA	regional health authority
RHOG	**Rural Home Ownership Grant**
RIBA	**Royal Institute of British Architects**
RICS	**Royal Institution of Chartered Surveyors**
RPI	**Retail Price Index**
RSF	**Rent Surplus Fund**
RSG	**Revenue Support Grant**
RSI	**Rough Sleepers Initiative**
RTB	**right to buy**
RTIA	**Receipts Taken Into Account**
RTM	**Rent to Mortgage**
RTM	**right to manage**
RTPI	**Royal Town Planning Institute**
Rate Fund Contribution	Former name for **General Fund Transfers**.
rateable value	An assessment of the annual rent which could be charged on a non-domestic property.
Rates	System of **local government** taxation which was replaced by the **Poll Tax** and then the **Council Tax**. The tax was incurred at a level determined by the property's **rateable value**.
reactive maintenance	See **response repairs**.
real return	Financial return on an investment expressed in **real terms**, ie with an adjustment for the effect of inflation.
real terms	Expression to describe an amount of money from which the effect of inflation has been excluded. Used to show changes in income or expenditure over time in **constant prices**.
reasonable	Term widely used in the law to describe behaviour based on sound judgment.

Receipts Taken Into Account	That portion of a **local authority's usable receipts** which are taken into consideration by **central government** when assessing each authority's **BCA** for the next financial year. In England **capital receipts** which come forward during the previous financial year are taken into account, whereas, in Wales, only those arising from the current year are considered.
recharges	Fees charged between departments within the same organisation for services, eg a **local authority's** legal, accountancy, personnel and public relations teams will recharge the housing department for work that it does on the department's behalf.
redemption	The repayment of a loan.
redemption yield	The return on a **security** at **redemption** including any capital gain less the purchase price and interest payments.
Redevelopment Area	Area of inner-city housing in Northern Ireland identified as needing large scale clearance and rebuilding.
red-lining	Excluding certain properties or areas from **mortgages**. It is alleged that many banks and **building societies** refuse to grant **mortgages** on certain types of housing, eg former **local authority** tower blocks, thus preventing the owners moving on.
referral	A recommendation from an agency to a housing provider that a particular household should be considered for accommodation. Many **local authorities** and **housing associations** have formal arrangements with social and health services for the referral of vulnerable households and individuals.
refinancing	Swapping one loan arrangement for another. Often done to take advantage of an alternative loan offered at a better rate.
regeneration	Improvement of a distinct geographic area by tackling a wide range of factors contributing to decline and hardship. Regeneration activities range from large-scale capital investment to small-scale community development projects.
regional allocation statement	Annual **Housing Corporation** statement of how each of its regional offices will distribute its allocation of funding in the current year. Produced in conjunction with the **regional policy statement**.
regional council	Scottish form of **county council**. Abolished under the **Local Government Review** and merged with **district councils** to form **unitary authorities** as from April 1996.
regional health authority	Public body with responsibility for providing health services in English health regions. England has 14 **RHAs** and they have a responsibility for providing a strategic framework for improving health levels within their region, often in conjunction with other agencies, such as housing departments and **housing associations**.
Regional Planning Guidance	Guidance from the **Secretary of State** providing a framework for the preparation of **structure plans** and **unitary development plans**. They were initially issued as **PPGs**. Key notes include:

RPG 6	– East Anglia
RPG 7	– Northern Region
RPG 8	– East Midlands
RPG 9	– South East
RPG 10	– South West
RPG 11	– West Midlands.

regional policy statement

Strategy document produced by each regional office of the **Housing Corporation** setting out its priorities for the allocation of funding in the next financial year.

registered charity

A charitable body which is registered in England & Wales with the **Charity Commission**, the registration of Scottish charities is administered by the **Scottish Office**.

registered housing association

A **housing association** which is registered with a **national housing agency**. Registration entitles an association to bid for **Social Housing Grant** (formerly **Housing Association Grant**) but requires that the association does not trade for profit and is established for the purpose of, or has among its **objects** or powers, the provision, construction, improvement or management of:

- houses for letting
- houses for occupation by **members** of the association, or
- **hostels**.

Essentially, all their **objects** must relate to the provision of housing. A registered housing association must also demonstrate that it is adequately controlled by its governing body (committee or **board of management**). Audited annual accounts must also be submitted to the **national housing agency** which has extensive powers of scrutiny over the association's affairs. Registered housing associations also qualify for **Section 62 tax relief** under the **Housing Associations Act 1985** and must adopt the **Tenants' Guarantee** in England & Wales.

Registered Rent

See **Fair Rent**.

registered social landlord

A **landlord** which is registered with the **national housing agency**. The term is introduced in England & Wales by the **Housing Act 1996** to reflect the expanded role of the **national housing agencies** as funders and regulators of new social **landlords** particularly **local housing companies**.

registered title

The registration of the details of a property at **HM Land Registry**. Each property has a separate title number and the register records the name of the owner, any **mortgagee** and details of any benefits, eg a right of way or **restrictive covenants** that relate to the property. Proof of ownership simply requires the production of a valid copy of the register held by **HM Land Registry**. Registration of title must be carried out whenever a property is sold, so that eventually the whole of England & Wales will have registered title.

Registers of Scotland

Government agency with responsibility for compiling the public register of land rights in Scotland. Performs many of the tasks of **HM Land Registry** in Scotland.

Registrar of Friendly Societies

Person with whom all **Industrial and Provident Societies** must register and to whom they must return audited annual accounts, make an annual return and notify of any rule changes. Most **registered housing associations** are also registered with the Registrar.

registration

Process through which **housing associations** and other **social landlords** go when seeking registration with the **national housing agency**.

regressive

Term used to describe a cost which hits the poorest hardest, ie it consumes a greater percentage of poorer household's income than richer one's. Often used in the context of taxation. The **Poll Tax** and **VAT** are both regressive, whilst Income Tax is **progressive** by virtue of the different tax bands.

regulated tenancy

Generic term for a **protected** or **statutory tenancy**.

regulatory review

Annual process of **Housing Corporation** reviewing the activities and performance of **registered housing associations**. Each of the other **national housing agencies** undertake similar tasks

rehabilitation

Restoration or renovation of a property in order to extend its useful life.

Renewal Area

An area of low quality housing, designated by a **local authority** following a **Neighbourhood Renewal Assessment**. A 10 year plan for renewal must be drawn up in partnership with local residents. **Central government** restrictions require 75% of the properties to be privately owned, 75 % to be **Unfit for Human Habitation** and 30% of local households to be dependent on **means tested** welfare benefits. Renewal Areas succeeded **General Improvement Areas** and **Housing Action Areas** when they were introduced in the **Local Government & Housing Act 1989**.

Rent Allowance

Housing Benefit paid to **housing association** and **private rented sector tenants**. Eligible **local authority tenants** receive **Rent Rebate**.

rent arrears

Unpaid outstanding rent payments. **Local authorities** are under a statutory duty to provide **performance indicators** on rent arrears to the **Audit Commission** (or **Accounts Commission** in Scotland).

rent assessment committee

Government appointed committee which acts as an appeal mechanism following a **rent officer's** assessment of **Fair Rents**. An **assured tenant** can also appeal to this committee where the **landlord** has served a notice of increase of rent and the **tenant** believes the proposed rent is above the **market rent**. The **Housing Act 1996** also transfers responsibility for dealing with disputes over **service charges** to the **RACs**.

rent bidding

The process by which **development** money is allocated to Welsh **housing associations** by **Tai Cymru** based on bids for their average rents for various sizes of property in different geographical areas.

rent deposit

An initial payment by a **tenant** to a **landlord** to cover the cost of any possible future unpaid rent or damage to the property.

rent guarantees	1) An assurance from a **local authority** to a private **landlord** to cover any defaulted payments which may arise on a **tenancy** eligible for **Housing Benefit**. This is a scheme to overcome problems **tenants** have in paying **rent deposits** and meeting rents before benefit payments are due.
	2) An assurance given by a **landlord** to its **tenants** about future rent rises.
rent guideline	See **guideline rent increase**.
rent modelling	Method of assessing the parameters which can be utilised to set rent levels.
rent officer	Individual with responsibility for setting **Fair Rents** for **tenants** under **protected tenancies**. The rent officer is also responsible for making a number of assessments relating to **Housing Benefit** applications for **private rented sector tenants** (and for **housing association tenants** at the **local authority's** discretion). The rent officer must determine whether the rent is significantly high in relation to other rents in the area, whether the dwelling exceeds the size criteria for the occupiers, whether the rent is exceptionally high for that dwelling, and the level of the **local reference rent**. The rent officer is also responsible for determining the amount of the rent attributable to services which are ineligible for **Housing Benefit**. Although the salaries of rent officers are usually paid by a **local authority** they carry out their responsibilities independently of the authority.
rent pooling	System of setting rents on the basis of loan charges, construction, management and maintenance costs across the whole of a **landlord's housing stock**. This means that **tenants** of the same **landlord** are charged rents according to the size and location of their home. In the absence of rent pooling, rents are calculated on the basis of the costs incurred by the particular estate or development which usually leads to wide variations in rent for similar properties owned by the same **landlord**.
Rent Rebate	**Housing Benefit** paid to **local authority tenants**. Eligible **housing association** and **private rented sector tenants** receive **Rent Allowance**. The rebate is paid in the form of a reduced rent bill.
Rent Rebate element of subsidy	The part of the subsidy from **central government** to local authorities to cover the costs of **Housing Benefit** for **local authority tenants**. Along with the **housing element of subsidy**, Rent Rebate subsidy goes to make up **local authorities' HRA subsidy**.
Rent Surplus Fund	**Housing association** money generated by surpluses they are deemed to be making under pre-1989 financial arrangements.
Rent to Mortgage	Government scheme to allow **local authority tenants** to buy an **equity sharing** arrangement, based on a payment equivalent to their current rent.
repayment mortgage	See **annuity mortgage**.

Report Stage	Time for the full House to consider amendments following **Committee Stage** of a **Bill**'s passage through Parliament.
repossession	Although different legal procedures apply, the term repossession is used to describe the process of either a **landlord** or **lender** (bank or **building society**) regaining control of a property. A **court order** for **possession** is needed to terminate **secure** and **assured tenancies** except when they have been **abandoned** or where the **tenant** surrenders the **tenancy** or gives **notice to quit** and leaves voluntarily.
reserved receipt	That portion of **capital receipts** which English & Welsh **local authorities** cannot spend, currently set at 75% for housing receipts and 50% for non-housing sources. The remainder is known as the **usable receipt**. Reserved receipts can be set-aside or used for paying off any debts the authority may have.
reserves	Money set aside by an organisation for future use. Their use may be specified, eg for debt servicing, or unspecified, eg to cover general future losses.
Resettlement Agency	Executive agency of the **DSS** responsible for transferring **homeless** persons **hostels** under government control to the voluntary sector.
residential home	Accommodation, registered with the **local authority**, to provide a home for dependent people with special care needs.
residual income	A measure of how much income remains after a household has met its housing costs. Used as an indicator for **affordable rents**, along with the **affordability ratio**.
residual mortgage	The amount of money a **housing association** must raise from private sources once the **HAG** allocation and resources from its own **reserves** have been deducted from the total cost of the project.
response maintenance	Repair works on **landlord's housing stock** which are conducted in response to **tenant** requests. They are generally minor faults, eg leaking pipes and faulty window latches, but unexpected large-scale works can also be classified as responsive, such as remedying storm damage, subsidence etc. Response maintenance is funded out of rental income or **service charges** and is also known as **day-to-day repairs** or **reactive maintenance**.
restrictive covenant	Part of a **conveyance** or **transfer** which restricts the use of land. These are sometimes used to ensure that **social housing** is provided on a particular plot.
restrictive procedure	Procedure laid down under **EU tendering** legislation allowing **local authorities** or other public bodies to select those organisations which will be invited to **tender** for a **contract**. Can be used in **CCT**.
Retail Price Index	Composite statistic used by the government to assess the rate of inflation.
retention sum	An amount of money withheld from a building **contractor** for the duration of the **defect liability period** as insurance against defects which are attributable to the **contractor**.

Revenue Contributions to Capital Outlay	Money taken from a revenue account, eg the **HRA** to finance **capital expenditure**. Rental income used to finance **capitalised repairs** are classified as **RCCOs**.
Revenue Deficit Grant	Grant to cover the assumed deficits of a **housing association** incurred on its pre-1989 stock.
revenue expenditure	Money spent on meeting the running costs of an organisation as opposed to **capital expenditure**.
Revenue Support Grant	Money paid by **central government** to **local authority's General Fund** to cover the **revenue expenditure** required to provide a standard level of service based on **SSAs**.
review	A reassessment of an applicant's welfare benefit entitlement by the same body as originally determined the claim.
right of re-entry	A right for a **landlord** to **repossess** a property let on a **fixed term tenancy** or **lease** because of a breach of the conditions of the **tenancy** or **lease** by the **tenant**, eg a failure to pay rent. In practice, the right of re-entry almost always has to be exercised by taking out **possession** proceedings which involves obtaining a **possession order**.
right to acquire	Generic name for **Housing Corporation** schemes to facilitate **housing association tenants** to purchase homes in the **owner-occupied** sector, eg **Voluntary Purchase Grant**, **Statutory Purchase Grant** and **Tenants' Incentive Scheme**.
right to buy	Programme of encouraging **tenants** to purchase their homes at a discounted rate. Although predominately associated with **local authority** housing, **secure tenants** of **non-charitable housing associations** are also eligible for the **right to buy** scheme if their homes were built using **HAG**.
right to compensation for improvements	Statutory compensation scheme for **secure tenants** who have made certain improvements to their home since April 1994. The compensation is paid when the **tenancy** ends and is calculated by a formula which discounts the cost of the improvements over their notional life. The minimum claim is £50 per claim whilst the maximum compensation payable is £3,000 per improvement.
right to exchange	Right conferred upon **secure tenants** and **assured tenants** of **housing associations** in England & Wales to exchange their home with a **secure tenant**. Both **tenants** must have the consent of their own **landlord** which can only be refused on the grounds of: • the **tenant** has been served with a **notice of seeking possession** or **possession** proceedings have begun • the size of the accommodation is not **reasonably** suitable to meet the needs of the other party • the home has facilities for a person with special needs and the **tenant** moving in to that home does not have such needs.
right to improve	Statutory right conferred upon **secure tenants** to carry out improvements to their home, subject to the written approval of their **landlord**. Consent cannot be **unreasonably** withheld. **Assured tenants** are usually given this right in their **tenancy agreement**.

right to manage	Entitlement of **tenants** to set up a **Tenant Management Organisation**. A **TMO** can take over responsibility for management of the **tenants'** homes from a **local authority** (or a **contractor** managing the housing under a **contract**), following two separate ballots of the **tenants**. **Section 16 grants** are available for **approved agencies** to assist **tenants** wishing to set up a **TMO** but the **local authority** must contribute 25% of the development costs. There is no equivalent in Scotland, but **local authorities** can set up **TMO** type bodies if they wish.
right to repair	A statutory right to compensation for **secure tenants** if certain small urgent repairs (costing less than £250) are not carried out within prescribed time limits.
ring-fencing	Restricting the use of specific categories of money to certain uses. The **HRA** is partially ring-fenced, preventing transfers from the **General Fund**.
room standard	A test used to assess whether a household is **statutorily overcrowded**. If two people of opposite sex over the age of 10 and not living together as partners have to share a bedroom then the room standard is contravened. For this purpose living rooms are considered to be an appropriate room for someone to sleep in.
ROP I/II	Right of Possession forms, which need to be served on any **secure tenant** which the **landlord** is seeking to **repossess**.
Rough Sleepers Initiative	Government funded scheme to provide short-term **hostel** places, permanent homes, private sector leases and winter shelters to people sleeping on the streets. The scheme also pays for outreach and resettlement services, all of which are delivered in conjunction with voluntary agencies. In March 1996, the scheme was extended to **local authorities** outside London who can demonstrate a need for such a programme.
Royal Assent	The final stage of a **Bill** becoming an **Act** at which the Crown gives assent to the new statute becoming law. It was last withheld in 1707.
Royal Commission on the Ancient & Historical Monuments of Scotland	Government body responsible for compiling, maintaining and curating the National Monuments Record of Scotland. The Commission provides advice and information for the preservation and conservation of such sites.
Royal Institution of Chartered Surveyors	Representative professional self-regulating body which supports chartered surveyors in their professional lives and enables them to share experience and knowledge.
Royal Town Planning Institute	Representative professional body of town planners, provides training to its members and promotes good practice as well as lobbying government.
RPI +/– X	The proposed formula by which **housing association** rents were to be restricted by the **Housing Corporation** in the **White Paper**, *Our Future Homes*. This proposal was designed to limit **housing association** rent rises to a factor X above or below the **Retail Price**

Index. Applications for **HAG** were to be assessed, partly, on the basis of rent levels in new developments in order to limit the future **Housing Benefit** costs to **central government**, but the introduction of the formula is currently shelved.

rural community council

County level charities working to promote the welfare of rural communities by encouraging community self-help, local initiatives and voluntary effort. They work in partnership with many organisations, including **local councils**.

Rural Development Commission

A government agency concerned with the economic and social well-being of people who live and work in the English countryside. Its activities include highlighting issues and raising awareness through research and the production of literature as well as influencing the main housing providers to ensure that rural housing problems are addressed.

Rural Home Ownership Grant

Grants available from **Scottish Homes** to individuals for the construction or renovation of properties in rural areas.

rural housing enablers

Independent people who act as catalysts and brokers to improve the supply of **affordable housing** in rural areas. Working closely with local communities, **local authorities**, **housing associations** and land-owners they assist in the assessment of **housing needs**, identifying suitable sites and help to facilitate the development process, ensuring the full involvement of the local community.

Rural Housing Forum

Alliance of organisations with an interest in rural housing issues. Members include **CIH, CPRE, ACRE, NFHA, HBF, ADC, Shelter** and the **Housing Corporation**.

Rural Housing Programme

A scheme run by the **Housing Corporation** since 1988 to target investment at villages below 3,000 in population for the provision of new low-cost homes.

Rural Voice

An alliance of national organisations which represent rural communities. Members include **ACRE** and **CPRE**.

S

SACRO	Scottish Association for the Care and Resettlement of Offenders
SAP	Standard Assessment Procedure
SAVE	A European initiative to promote **energy efficiency**, through technical measures and training in energy saving technologies.
SCA	Supplementary Credit Approval
SCG	Specified Capital Grants
SCORE	A **Continuous Recording of New Lettings** administered by the Scottish Federation of Housing Associations.
SCSH	Scottish Council for Single Homeless
SEPA	Scottish Environment Protection Agency
SFHA	Scottish Federation of Housing Associations
SHAC	Independent housing aid centre which has been taken over by **Shelter**.
SHACT	Scottish Housing Associations Charitable Trust
SHCS	Scottish House Condition Survey
SHG	Social Housing Grant
SHIL	Single Homelessness In London. An all party political group set up by the London boroughs to bring together statutory and voluntary sector organisations involved in providing services to single **homeless** people in London. SHIL aims to encourage the development of good standard temporary and permanent accommodation and related support services for **homeless** people. SHIL undertakes research, produces reports and lobbies relevant bodies to achieve its aims.
SHMG	Social Housing Management Grant
SI	Statutory Instrument
SITRA	A voluntary organisation and registered charity that offers training, consultancy and advice to providers of **special needs housing** in the **social housing** sector.
SLA	service level agreement
SLGIU	Scottish Local Government Information Unit
SMG	Supplementary Management Grant
SNAP	Special Needs Allowance Package
SNCG	Special Needs Capital Grant
SNMA	Special Needs Management Allowance
SODD	Scottish Office Development Department

SPED	Scheme for the Purchase of Evacuated Dwellings
SPPA	Special Projects Promotional Allowance
SPPPS	Scheme for the Purchase of Properties in the Private Sector
SPPR	Scheme for the Purchase of Properties for Rehabilitation
SPPSD	Scheme for the Purchase of Private Sector Dwellings
SRB	Single Regeneration Budget
SSA	Standard Spending Assessment
SSAC	Social Security Advisory Committee
SSAP	Standard Statement of Accounting Practice
SSHA	Scottish Special Housing Association
SSSI	Site of Special Scientific Interest
STO	Scottish Tenants' Organisation
SURI	Small Urban Renewal Initiatives
SWSG	Social Work Services Group
Safe Neighbourhoods Unit	Independent organisation that specialises in housing research, consultation and participation, estate and high rise management, safety and security as well as waste recycling.
schedule of rates	Price list of construction work, used to determine the cost of a **contract** for building work.
schedule of rates contract	A **contract** which allows modules of work to be done at pre-determined rates.
scheme development standards	Construction standard set down by the **Housing Corporation** to which all **housing associations' developments** must conform.
Scheme for the Purchase of Evacuated Dwellings	Northern Ireland scheme to purchase homes which people have had to flee as a result of violence or intimidation. The properties are purchased at market rates and absorbed into the **NIHE** stock or resold.
Scheme for the Purchase of Private Sector Dwellings	**NIHE** scheme to purchase private sector dwellings to provide housing for families displaced by civil unrest.
Scheme for the Purchase of Properties for Rehabilitation	**NIHE** scheme to purchase derelict private sector homes for rehabilitation.
Scheme for the Purchase of Properties in the Private Sector	**NIHE** scheme to re-house families displaced by redevelopment for whom there is no available housing. Used to speed up the clearance and redevelopment process.

Scope	National charity that provides information and support for people with cerebral palsy and their families. It also campaigns on wider disability issues. Formerly known as the Spastics Society.
Scottish Association for the Care and Resettlement of Offenders	Scottish equivalent of **NACRO**.
Scottish block	Amount of public expenditure available to the **Scottish Office** from the Budget.
Scottish Building Contracts	Standard **contracts** for use in Scotland based on **JCT contracts**.
Scottish Council for Single Homeless	Campaign group in Scotland which exists to promote awareness about single **homelessness**, identify and promote ways of alleviating **homelessness** and work with appropriate agencies and individuals to tackle single **homelessness**. It is the Scottish equivalent of **CHAR**.
Scottish Environment Protection Agency	A **Scottish Office quango** responsible for regulating pollution from industry, homes and agriculture. It succeeds the River Purification Boards, Her Majesty's Industrial Pollution Inspectorate and **local authority** environmental health departments' pollution control and waste regulation functions.
Scottish Federation of Housing Associations	The body which represents the views of **housing associations** in negotiations on housing policy with government and other bodies. It promotes, encourages and assists the formation of **housing associations**, providing support, advice and training to help them operate. It has counterparts in each of the other countries of the UK – the **Welsh**, **Northern Ireland** and **National Federation of Housing Associations**.
Scottish Homes	The **national housing agency** in Scotland. It combines a wide range of functions, including promoting all forms of housing, regulating and funding **housing associations** as well as managing a stock of properties. Scottish Homes also sponsors an extensive research programme and pilots innovative housing solutions.
Scottish House Condition Survey	Scottish equivalent of the **English**, **Welsh** and **Northern Ireland House Condition Surveys**.
Scottish Housing Associations Charitable Trust	Scottish equivalent of **HACT**.
Scottish Local Government Information Unit	Scottish counterpart to the **LGIU**.
Scottish National Housing & Town Planning Institute	Scottish **NHTPC**.

Scottish Office	**Central government** department which overseas Scottish affairs headed by the **Secretary of State** for Scotland.
Scottish Office Development Department	Section of the **Scottish Office** with responsibility for planning, housing, regeneration and **local government**.
Scottish Special Housing Association	Scottish **housing associations** set up by the government to supplement the work of **housing associations** in Scotland. Amalgamated with the **Housing Corporation** in Scotland to form **Scottish Homes**.
Scottish Tenants' Organisation	Umbrella organisation for **tenants' associations** in Scotland.
Second Reading	First substantive stage of a **Bill's** passage through Parliament. It usually occurs two weeks after the **First Reading** and allows the House to consider the principle of the **Bill**.
secondary housing association (or co-operative)	A **housing association** or **co-operative** which does not directly provide accommodation, but facilitates and encourages other associations or supplies advice and other housing-related services.
Secretary of State	Government minister in charge of a **central government** department and with a place in the Cabinet, eg Secretary of State for the Environment.
Section 9 consent	Consent given under the **Housing Associations Act 1985** by the **Housing Corporation** and **Tai Cyrmu** to allow a **housing association** to dispose of a property. Subject to change in the **Housing Act 1996**.
Section 13 notice	A notice issued by the **Secretary of State** under the **Local Government Act 1988**, requiring a **local authority** to explain its **tendering** procedure in the light of allegations of **anti-competitive behaviour** or any other aspect of the handling of **contracts** awarded under **CCT**.
Section 14 notice	A notice issued by the **Secretary of State** under the **Local Government Act 1988**, setting out the action that the **local authorities** are required to take as a result of the investigations carried out into allegations of **anti-competitive behaviour** or other defects in the **CCT** process.
Section 15	Section of the **Housing Associations Act 1985** which prohibits any payments or benefits being made to **board members**, former **board members**, close relatives of **board members**, or businesses in which **board members** are involved.
Section 16 grant	Grants provided by the **Secretary of State** to **approved agencies** under Section 16 of the **Housing & Planning Act 1986** to promote **tenant participation** and to develop **Tenant Management Organisations** in **local authority** housing.
Section 17 appointments	Under Section 17 of the **Housing Associations Act 1985**, the **national housing agency** can appoint an individual to the **board of**

management of a **registered housing association** in certain circumstances.

Section 25 consent

Permission from the **Secretary of State** for a **local authority** to provide financial assistance under Section 25 of the **Local Government Act 1988** to an organisation or individual to enable them to acquire, construct, convert, improve, maintain or manage property which is intended to be privately let as accommodation.

Section 28 enquiry

An enquiry set up under powers conferred upon the **national housing agency** by the **Housing Associations Act 1985** allowing them to investigate a **registered housing association** where there is a suspicion of misconduct or mismanagement.

Section 54 tax relief

See **Corporation Tax**.

Section 62 tax relief

Grant payable under certain circumstances to **registered housing associations** to reimburse them for Income Tax and **Corporation Tax** liabilities.

Section 73 grant

Funding available to voluntary organisations providing services for **homeless** people.

Section 80 notice

A notice issued by a **local authority's** environmental health department requiring occupiers to stop activities that are causing a **statutory nuisance** or requiring owners or **leaseholders** to carry out works to prevent the premises being a **statutory nuisance**.

Section 87 grant

Grants provided by the **Housing Corporation** and **Tai Cymru** under Section 87 of the **Housing Associations Act 1985,** but amended in the **Housing Act 1996**. The money is available to facilitate the proper performance of **registered social landlords**.

Section 106 agreement

A **planning obligation** between a developer and the local planning authority under the **Town & Country Planning Act 1990**, which makes planning approval conditional on certain requirements. For example, **local authorities** can make approval of a planning application dependent on the provision of a quantity of affordable housing or social infrastructure development or finance towards that end.

secure tenancy

Most **tenancies** created by **local authorities, New Town** Corporations, **Housing Action Trusts** and **Urban Development Corporations** fall within the definition of a secure tenancy under the **Housing Act 1985 (Housing (Scotland) Act 1987)**. Before 15 January 1989 (1/1/89 in Scotland), **housing associations** also issued secure tenancies but since that date almost all have been **assured tenancies**. A **tenancy** ceases to be a secure tenancy if the **tenant** no longer occupies the dwelling as her or his only or principal home. A secure tenant is entitled to remain a **tenant** unless a **court order for possession** is made against them. **Possession** can only be obtained where **grounds for possession** exist. These include:
- failure to pay the rent
- where the **tenant** or a person living with the **tenant** has caused a **nuisance** or annoyance to neighbours

- breach of **tenancy** conditions
- conviction for using the property for immoral or illegal purposes
- making a false statement in order to get the **tenancy**
- damage to furniture or the dwelling
- where the dwelling is required to be vacant so that major works can be carried out.

In most cases the court only grants **possession** if it considers it **reasonable**. In some cases alternative accommodation has to be provided. Secure **tenants** also qualify for the:

- **right to buy** after 2 years in residence
- **right to repair** their home
- right to **sub-let** with their **landlord's** consent and to take in **lodgers**
- right to **assign** the tenancy in certain circumstances
- **right to exchange** with other secure **tenants** and **housing association assured tenants**
- right to **succession** for spouses and family members
- right to consultation on a range of issues (not in Scotland)
- right to information about their **tenancies**
- **right to improve** with their **landlord's** consent and the **right to compensation for improvements** when the tenancy ends in certain circumstances
- **right to manage**
- right to vote before their homes are transferred to a private sector **landlord**
- right to be consulted about the terms of any **management agreement** (including a **contract** let under **CCT)** and about the identity of the person who is to be the manager under any agreement.

Secured By Design
A police initiative to endorse **developments** which adopt security guidelines in new and refurbished homes and commercial premises.

security
A term with many meanings and uses, three of which are:
1) generic term for a means of investing money, eg a share or a **bond**.
2) a pledge of financial or physical property which will be surrendered upon failure to repay a loan
3) **security of tenure**.

security of tenure
Rights given to some **tenants** which prevent the **landlord** regaining **possession** unless the **landlord** can prove to a court that there are **grounds for possession** which are set out in **Acts of Parliament**, eg for **secure tenants** in England & Wales, they are set out in the **Housing Act 1985**.

seed corn grant
Funds given by **Scottish Homes** to set up a new **housing association** or **co-operative**.

Select Committee
A parliamentary committee of MPs or Lords with the capacity to investigate and report on matters within their remit. There are different types of committee, they may be:
- departmental – shadow the activities of the relevant government, department eg **Environment Select Committee**

- service – internal parliamentary issues, eg catering or broadcasting
- or, they may preside on issues of general parliamentary interest, eg the Committee on Members' Interests or the Committee of Privileges.

self-build
Movement which promotes and facilitates the building of properties by prospective occupants.

service charge
A sum payable by a **tenant** to a **landlord** (or by a **leaseholder** to a **freeholder**) under the terms of a **tenancy** (or **lease**) which is paid in addition to the **rent**. Service charges are used to separately identify the cost of some services, eg **warden** service, **concierge**, cleaning of common parts, lighting of common parts, repairs, ground maintenance, etc. Different **tenancies** and **leases** have different arrangements for the kind of costs that will be included within the service charge and **Housing Benefit** is only payable on specific elements of a service charge.

service contract
Generic term for a **contract** between two parties which specifies the delivery of a service.

service level agreement
Semi-formal agreement between two departments in an organisation covering services to be provided by one to the other.

service provider
Organisation or individual charged with responsibility for providing a public service.

set-aside
Money from **capital receipts** which **local authorities** must keep in reserve to cover debts. Currently **local authorities** must set aside 75% of **capital receipts** from the sale of housing. Also known as **reserved receipts**.

Severe Disablement Allowance
A **non-contributory** equivalent of **Incapacity Benefit** for severely disabled people.

Severe Hardship Payments
A discretionary payment of **Job Seeker's Allowance** to prevent a claimant becoming destitute. Aimed at those who are otherwise ineligible for welfare benefits, such as those aged under 18.

share capital
Capital raised by an organisation through the issuing and selling of shares in itself.

shared housing
Housing in which individuals live separately, but with shared kitchen and bathroom facilities. **Hostels** and **group homes** fall into this category.

shared ownership
Low cost home-ownership concept which allows occupants of property to purchase only part of their home whilst paying rent on the remainder.

shared-ownership lease
A **lease** under which the **leaseholder** can purchase part of the **leasehold** and continue to pay rent on the remainder. Greater proportions of the **leasehold** interest can be bought at later dates reducing the amount of rent that is payable; this is known as **staircasing**.

Shelter	The national campaign for **homeless** people. Shelter campaigns to prevent **homelessness** through a network of advice centres and for an economically sustainable housing system which provides safe, secure and affordable homes for all. There are also sister organisations in Scotland & Wales. Shelter (Scotland) is a division of Shelter whilst Shelter (Cymru) is a separate organisation.
sheltered housing	Term with a wide variety of meanings, generally accepted elements are that it is designed specifically for people with support needs often including some form of emergency alarm system and on site or **peripatetic** support.
sheriff officers	Scottish **bailiff** for the Sheriff Court.
short assured tenancy	Scottish equivalent of an **assured shorthold tenancy**. Contrary to the post **Housing Act 1996** position in England & Wales, unless the **tenant** is explicitly informed that the tenancy is a short assured it will be an **assured tenancy**.
short-life housing	Generally, properties with an expected life of between 2 and 10 years.
short-term lease	A **lease** which is limited to a short time period, eg 3 years. **Local authority** and **housing associations** often take out short-term leases on private properties in order to temporarily overcome housing shortages.
SI 1992/512	See **accounting order**.
silent renewal	The renewal of a **tenancy** without any actions on behalf of the **landlord** or the **tenant**. In the absence of **periodic tenancies** in Scotland, **tenancies** are regularly renewed through silent renewal. Also known as **tacit relocation**.
Single Regeneration Budget	Unified scheme for distributing government funds for **regeneration** including housing. Bids are competitively assessed and emphasis is placed on partnership between **local authorities** and other organisations. Among other programmes, it replaces **Urban Development Corporations**, **Urban Programme**, **Estate Action**, **City Challenge** and **Housing Action Trusts**.
sinking funds	Financial provision for a **liability** at some stage in the future, eg the finance of major repairs or the repayment of a debt.
Site of Special Scientific Interest	An area identified by **English Nature** and designated by the **local authority** and **central government** where development is restricted in the pursuit of nature conservation.
sitting tenant	A person who is already a **tenant,** when the property is transferred to a new **landlord**.
Size Related Rent	An assessment by a **rent officer** of the **market rent** which would be payable if the claimant did not occupy accommodation which is larger than they need. It is used to determine the **Appropriate Rent**.
Small Landlords' Association	National organisation for **private rented sector landlords** of residential property. Provides guidance to members in all matters relating to the **private rented sector**.

Smaller Urban Renewal Initiatives	Scottish scheme aimed at regenerating localities through a partnership between **local authorities**, community groups and the private sector.
snagging	The process of highlighting any outstanding work in a building **contract**.
Social Fund	A system of one-off payments administered by the **Benefits Agency** which includes **Community Care Grant**, **Crisis Loans** and **Budgeting Loans**.
social housing	Loosely defined term which refers to housing provided at **affordable rents** by a publicly accountable **landlord**. **Housing associations, Housing Action Trusts, local authorities, local housing companies** are all examples of social housing providers.
social housing agreement	An agreement drawn up between **local authorities** and some or all of the other **social housing** providers operating in an area which is used as the basis for a **common housing register**. The agreement is likely to cover issues such as the terms of partnership, mutual initiatives and agreed performance expectations.
Social Housing Grant	Under the **Housing Act 1996, Housing Association Grant** in England & Wales is replaced by Social Housing Grant, to reflect the **national housing agency's** new powers of regulation and funding over organisations with **approved landlord status**, including **local housing companies**.
Social Housing Management Grant	New title for **Special Needs Management Allowance** following the **Housing Act 1996**.
Social Security Advisory Committee	**DSS quango** which provides advice on policy issues confronting the Department. The **Secretary of State** is under a duty to consult the **SSAC** before changing benefit regulations.
social security benefits	Those welfare benefits which are administered by the **Benefits Agency** on behalf of the **DSS**. These include **Income Support, Unemployment Benefit, Disability Living Allowance, Attendance Allowance** etc. **Housing Benefit** and **Council Tax** Benefit are not social security benefits as they are administered by the **local authority**.
Social Work Services Group	Section of the **Scottish Office** with responsibility for, among other things, **Care in the Community**.
space standard	A test used to assess whether a household is **statutorily overcrowded**. The maximum number of persons permitted before the household contravenes the space standard is laid out in Section 326 of the **Housing Act 1985**.
Special Needs Allowance Package	Money available in Scotland to cover the running costs of **special needs housing**. It is the Scottish equivalent of **SNMA**.
Special Needs Capital Grant	Capital funding available from **Scottish Homes** to encourage the building or renovating of **supported housing** by the private sector or voluntary organisations.

special needs housing	Term with a wide variety of meanings. Its loosest definition is housing which aims to meet the needs of people who are deemed to have particular needs that cannot be met through ordinary housing. Special needs housing comes in a variety of forms, **hostels, mobility housing, wheelchair housing, move-on accommodation** etc.
Special Needs Management Allowance	Funding available to **registered housing associations** to cover the **revenue expenditure** incurred by **special needs housing** projects. To be replaced with **Social Housing Management Grant** following the **Housing Act 1996**.
Special Projects Promotional Allowance	**HAG** funding for **registered housing associations** developing special needs projects.
Special Transitional Grant	**Central government** money available to **local authorities** to provide residential/nursing placements and community-based packages of care.
Specified Capital Grants	**Central government** money available to **local authorities** mainly for improving private sector properties in their locality. It forms part of the **HIP** allocation and is determined according to stock profiles and data on renovation costs.
squatter/squat	A person who is occupying accommodation illegally without the permission of anyone who is legally entitled to give permission. A squatter is committing a **trespass**. Court action for **repossession** can be taken and a temporary **possession order** (interim **possession order**) can be obtained within a few days in most cases. A squatter commits a criminal offence if s/he fails to leave the property within 24 hours of being served with an interim **possession order**. **Mesne profits** can be claimed from a squatter as compensation for illegal occupation of the property.
staff grid	Management technique used to evaluate the cost of employing individual members of staff.
staircasing	Process by which **shared ownership** households can increase (or reduce) the ownership proportion of the stake in their home.
stamp duty	One-off tax payable by home buyers upon purchase of their home. Currently set at 1% of the sale price on properties over £60,000.
Standard Assessment Procedure	**Central government** initiative to produce a means of comparison between **NHER** and **Starpoint**. Both schemes are now obliged to give a **SAP** rating (in addition to their own) on a scale of 1-100. It is intended to reduce confusion and promote the widespread use of energy ratings.
Standard Spending Assessment	**Central government** assessment of how much **revenue expenditure** each **local authority** should spend in order to provide a standard level of service. Used to distribute the **RSG** to **local authority**. **Housing Revenue Accounts** expenditure is separate from this process.

Standard Statement of Accounting Practice	A statement attached to an organisation's accounts indicating the method by which the accounts were compiled.
Standing Committee	A parliamentary committee appointed to consider a particular **Bill** clause by clause, during the **Committee Stage** of its passage through Parliament.
Starpoint	Counterpart energy rating system to **NHER**. Buildings are assessed on criteria including design, orientation, size and heating system. Each is awarded a star rating between 1 (very inefficient) and 5 (very efficient). See **Standard Assessment Procedure (SAP)**.
starter homes	Housing intended for small and newly formed families. They tend to have only one bedroom, but may provide scope for extension at a later date.
starts	Number of buildings started over a period of time.
statutorily overcrowded	Under the **Housing Act 1985**, households are considered to be living in overcrowded conditions if they fail the **room standard** or the **space standard**.
statutory housing register	The **housing register** which all **local authorities** must keep by law. The **Housing Act 1996** lays down those categories of applicant who should receive priority in **allocations** and restrictions on who should and should not be included on the register. If the **local authority** is a member of a **common housing register** it must be able to separate those applicants on the statutory list from all others.
statutory form of accounts	Certain organisations are legally bound to produce their accounts in a certain format, generically referred to as a statutory form of accounts, eg the format of **registered housing associations'** accounts is set out in **SI 1992/512**, also known as the **accounting order**.
Statutory Instrument	Regulation put forward by ministers and approved by Parliament. Such regulations can only be made if they are allowed within the relevant **Act of Parliament**.
statutory nuisance	Defined in England & Wales in the **Environmental Protection Act 1990** and the Environmental Health Act (Scotland) 1995 as: • accumulations or deposits • smoke, gas, fumes or noise emitted from premises • nuisance arising from the place or manner in which an animal is kept • or generally the state of premises which are prejudicial to health or a nuisance. These provisions can be used to deal with barking dogs, noisy parties and smoky bonfires. Action is initiated against the person responsible for the **nuisance** by the **local authority** serving a **Section 80 notice**.
Statutory Purchase Grant	New scheme launched in the **Housing Act 1996**, requiring English & Welsh **housing associations** to offer **tenants** in dwellings built with **SHG** the opportunity to purchase their homes at a discounted rate in much the same way as **right to buy** operates. **Registered social**

landlords will be required to **ring-fence** the **capital receipts** and use them to replace the homes they sell. The **Secretary of State** for the Environment has discretion to exempt villages with fewer than 3,000 dwellings, whilst the **Secretary of State** for Wales has the power to exempt areas with low population densities.

statutory tenancy

A **tenancy** created by statute which comes into existence when a **protected tenancy** has been brought to an end. A statutory tenancy also arises on the death of a **protected tenant** if there is a person qualified to **succeed** to the **tenancy**. The terms of the statutory tenancy are the same as the **protected tenancy** which preceded it. The **tenant** has **security of tenure** and the **landlord** can only get **possession** when there are **grounds for possession**. In Scotland, a **notice to quit** is generally required to create a statutory tenancy and they can be created from **assured** as well as **protected tenancies**.

staying-put

Concept designed to allow elderly home owners to stay in their homes as they grow older whilst having their ever increasing support needs met. Staying-put schemes tend to include three elements:
- a counselling service to help people choose a solution which meets their needs
- financial advice and assistance
- assistance with **adaptations**.

stock condition survey

A survey which assesses the fabric of dwellings. It concentrates on the physical elements of a building such as heating facilities, disrepair, ventilation, dampness and stability.

stock rationalisation

An initiative stimulated by **Tai Cymru** to encourage Welsh **housing associations** to exchange stock with each other in order to form more easily managed **housing stock**.

stock transfer

Transfer of ownership and management of **local authority housing stock** to a **housing association, Housing Action Trust** or **local housing company**, eg **Large Scale Voluntary Transfer** or **partial transfer**.

strategic enabling role

The provision of a strategy for meeting **housing needs** from a variety of sources. This is promoted by the government as the future role for **local authorities.** Instead of concentrating solely on managing their own **housing stock**, authorities will concentrate on assessing **housing need** and the required resources in their area and promote and facilitate partnerships between a range of local housing providers including **private rented sector landlords, housing associations** and private **developers**.

strategic review

Process of evaluating an organisation's services, stock, personnel and objectives with a view to defining future changes.

stress area

See **designated stress area**.

structural deficit

A measure of budgetary deficit after correcting for cyclical effects.

Structural Funds

See **European Structural Fund**.

structure plan	**Development plan** produced by **county councils** which sets out their strategic planning policies.
sub-lease	See **sub-tenancy**.
sub-let	An agreement under which a person who is the **tenant** grants a **tenancy** to another person whilst retaining their own **tenancy**. The **tenant** who grants the **tenancy** becomes the **landlord** under the new **tenancy** and the new **tenant** is called a **sub-tenant**. Under the **Housing Act 1985 (Housing (Scotland) Act 1987)**, **secure tenants** have the right to sub-let part of their homes with their **landlord's** consent (which cannot be **unreasonably** withheld). If a **secure tenant** sub-lets the whole of their home, the **tenancy** ceases to be a **secure tenancy**. Under the **Tenants' Guarantee**, **housing associations** in England & Wales are required to give the same rights to **assured tenants** and most have this written in to their **tenancy agreements**. Many **local authorities** and **housing associations** are sympathetic to **tenants** who temporarily leave the area fully intending to return and wish to sub-let their properties in the meantime.
sub-tenancy	A **tenancy** outlining the conditions of possession in a **sub-let** between a **tenant** and a **sub-tenant**. The **tenancy** between the **tenant** acting as **landlord** and the actual **landlord** is known as the **head-tenancy**. Also known as **sub-lease**.
sub-tenant	The **tenant** in a **sub-tenancy** (or **lease**) arrangement. For example, a person who **sub-lets** a **local authority** or **housing association tenant's** home is a sub-tenant.
succession	The automatic transfer of a **tenancy** on the death of a **tenant**. Succession to **secure tenancies** if a spouse survives the **tenant** and was living with the **tenant** at the time of the **tenant's** death. Succession can take place to other family members if they were living with the **tenant** for a year before the death. Succession can only occur once under **secure** and **assured tenancies** and twice in the case of **protected tenancies**. When a **joint tenant** dies, the **tenancy** continues and the survivor(s) automatically remain as **tenant**(s), but when the surviving **tenant** dies the previous death counts as if it had been a succession.
Supplementary Credit Approval	**Central government** permission for **local authorities** to extend borrowing for **capital expenditure** beyond their **Basic Credit Approval**. SCAs are usually given for specific projects part way through the financial year.
Supplementary Management Grant	Top-up funding from the **Housing Corporation** to cover the higher costs small **housing associations** incur when providing **move-on accommodation**.
supported housing	Housing with which the resident receives support to enable them to live independently in the community. Supported housing is often developed to meet the needs of a particular group of people with **special needs**, eg young people leaving care.
surety bond	A **bond** taken out by a **landlord** to cover the costs incurred should a **contractor** not complete the terms of a **contract**. Usually taken out by

	housing associations as insurance against the possibility of escalating **development** costs. Also known as a **contract guarantee bond**.
surrender	An agreement between **landlord** and **tenant** to bring a **tenancy** to an end. In some cases, the actions of the **tenant** may suggest that they want to end the **tenancy**, eg because they have **abandoned** the property and this may give rise to an **implied surrender**. In other cases a surrender is signed.
suspended court order	A **court order** that does not come into effect provided certain conditions are complied with, eg a suspended **possession order** for **rent arrears** usually does not come into effect provided the **tenant** pays the current rent and a weekly sum off the arrears and court costs.
sustainable development	A term with no fixed or universally agreed definition, however consensus appears to centre around the **Brundtland Report** which focuses on 'development that meets the needs of the present without compromising the ability of future generations to meet their own needs'.
sustainable growth	Like **sustainable development**, there is no fixed or universally agreed definition but any plan based on the concept would need to incorporate the four principles of sustainability: futurity, environment, equity and participation.
SWOT Analysis	Strengths, weaknesses, opportunities and threats analysis, used in business planning.
system built	Building construction techniques which rely on factory-built components which are assembled on site, eg pre-cast concrete tower blocks.

TAN	Technical Advice Note
TCI	Total Cost Indicators
TDS	Transferable Discount Scheme
TEAS	Tenants' Energy Advice Service
TEC	Training and Enterprise Council
THFC	Housing Finance Corporation (The)
TIES	Totally Integrated Energy Solution
TIS	Tenants' Incentive Scheme
TMO	Tenant Management Organisation
TMV	Tenanted Market Value
TOPS	Tenant Ownership Purchase Scheme
TPAS	Tenant Participation Advisory Service
TQM	Total Quality Management

tacit relocation
The **silent renewal** of a **tenancy**. In the absence of **periodic tenancies** in Scotland, **tenancies** are regularly renewed through tacit relocation.

Tai Cymru
The **national housing agency** for Wales. Tai Cymru is a **Welsh Office** agency with responsibility for promoting the **housing association** movement, regulating their activities and administering funding for building and renovation programmes. The **Housing Corporation** and **Scottish Homes** are its English and Scottish counterparts. Also known as **Housing for Wales**.

taper
Rate at which **Housing Benefit** and **Family Credit** is withdrawn from claimants as their income rises.

target hardening
An approach to crime prevention which attempts to reduce the vulnerability of particular targets to vandalism and theft. Elements of the approach include better locks, stronger doors, phone entry systems and minimalist public utilities such as telephones.

Tariff Income
An assumed income of a benefit claimant based on their **assets** and savings. This is added to the actual income to assess their eligibility for **Housing Benefit** and **Family Credit** claims.

Task Force on Government Departments' Empty Homes
A government body set up in 1992 and established to oversee an agreed programme of disposal of government owned empty homes to be brought back into use for people in **housing need**.

Technical Advice Note
A supplement to a **PPG** which elaborates on the details of the guidance.

tenancy	Permission to occupy a property with **exclusive possession** on certain conditions, usually including the payment of rent. Permission is given by a person who is entitled to possession of the property who is called the **landlord**. In some cases, the **landlord** will own the freehold. In other cases, the **landlord** may also be a **tenant** under another tenancy in which case the tenancy to the **landlord** is known as the **head-tenancy** and the tenancy granted by the **landlord** is known as a **sub-tenancy**. A tenancy may be for a fixed period (ie a **fixed term tenancy**) or for a period which continues indefinitely until notice is given to bring it to an end (ie a **periodic tenancy**). The term tenancy is interchangeable with the term **lease** but tenancy tends to be used for shorter-term arrangements. There are many different types of tenancy including **secure tenancies**, **assured tenancies**, **assured shorthold tenancies** and **protected tenancies**.
tenancy agreement	The agreement (or **contract**) under which a **landlord** lets property to a **tenant**. It is usually in written form.
tenancy turnover	The rate at which **tenancies** change. Usually expressed as the number of households who have inhabited a dwelling since its construction (or over a fixed period of time).
tenant	Individual or organisation who is renting property under a **lease** or **tenancy**. It includes people renting homes from **local authorities**, **housing associations** and in the **private rented sector**. The term tenant can be used to cover anyone who holds a **lease** and is interchangeable with **leaseholder** and with **lessee**. However, the term **leaseholder** tends to be used only to describe individuals who have bought flats under long **leases** (eg of 125 years) or under **shared ownership** schemes and the term **lessee** tends to be used in business **leases**.
Tenant Management Co-operative	Form of **TMO** in which all **tenants** on an estate can become **members**. The management committee is usually made up of only **members**. **Local authority** representatives and councillors may be on the board but do not usually have voting rights. **TMOs** may alternatively be **Estate Management Boards**.
Tenant Management Organisations	Voluntary bodies set up to run the management functions of an estate, usually under the **right to manage**. TMOs have to be **Industrial and Provident Societies**. They can take many forms, two of the commonest are **Tenant Management Co-operatives** and **Estate Management Boards**. Their responsibilities often include: • new lettings • day-to-day repairs and maintenance • cleaning and care-taking • dealing with neighbour disputes • collecting rents and chasing arrears • ensuring **tenant** representation • employing staff to carry out these functions • managing and controlling the budget for management and maintenance. **Section 16 grant** is available to cover the costs of setting up a **TMO**.
Tenant Ownership Purchase Scheme	Scottish version of the **Voluntary Purchase Grant** scheme.

tenant participation

A two way process involving sharing information and ideas, where **tenants** are able to influence and take part in what is happening. **Landlords** pursuing **tenant** participation should seek **tenants'** views when making decisions and explain decisions to **tenants**. **Tenants** should have the right and genuine opportunities to make and influence decisions on a full range of issues.

Tenant Participation Advisory Service

Independent voluntary organisation with membership open to **local authorities**, **housing associations** and **tenants'** organisations. **TPAS** provides help, advice, information, research and training to **tenants** and **landlords** on all aspects of **tenant participation** and involvement in housing and regeneration issues. **TPAS** is divided into three organisations: TPAS (England), TPAS (Wales) and TPAS (Scotland).

Tenanted Market Value

The **net present value** of a property with **sitting tenants**. The flow of rental income and expenditure on management and maintenance over a 30 year period are taken into consideration. The **TMV** is used in the valuation of **LSVT** properties.

tenants' association

Voluntary body of **tenants** representing the views of its membership and local residents to their **landlord,** the **local authority** and any other relevant agencies.

Tenants' Charter

A part of the **Citizen's Charter** initiative which outlines the level of service **local authority tenants** should expect from their **landlord** and the responsibilities that are placed upon them.

Tenants' Choice (England & Wales)

Government scheme offering **tenants** of **local authorities, New Town** Development Corporations and **Housing Action Trusts** the right to conduct a ballot to decide on transferring the management of their estate to another **landlord**. Potential **landlords** must have **approved landlord status** and can bid to take over an estate. Voting in the ballot is on a negative basis – failure to vote is counted as a yes vote, therefore 50% of eligible **tenants** actually have to vote no to prevent the transfer taking place. The **Housing Act 1996** brings to an end this scheme, which has run with limited success since 1988.

Tenants' Choice (Scotland)

Like **Tenants' Choice** in England & Wales, this scheme allows **tenants** to transfer to organisations with **approved landlord status**, however, in Scotland it is individual **tenants** who transfer, rather than whole estates, consequently there are no ballots.

Tenants' Energy Advice Service

Organisation which provides free technical support to **tenants' associations** in London with heating and fuel cost problems.

Tenants' Guarantee

Housing Corporation and **Tai Cymru** statement of the rights **housing association periodic assured tenants** can expect, including a specification of the level of service they should receive.

Tenants' Incentive Scheme

Housing Corporation programme providing cash sums to encourage **housing association tenants** to purchase homes on the open market and so freeing up their present home for others in **housing need**.

tender

Formal offer to provide a service at a certain price which, if accepted, forms a binding **contract**.

tender documents	Documents for prospective tenderers outlining the service for which they are to bid.
tender evaluation model	Technique for selecting and evaluating **tenders**.
tenement	Terraced block of walk-up flats, usually built in the Victorian period and mainly associated with Scotland.
tenure	With respect to housing, tenure indicates the status of a person who occupies housing. The main forms of housing tenure are: • **freehold** (ie ownership) • **leasehold** (eg the status of a person who owns a 125 year **lease**) • **tenancy** (eg the status of a **housing association**, **local authority** or **private rented sector tenant**) • **licence** (eg some residents of **hostels** and family members of **tenants** or owners). Those who own the **freehold** or a **leasehold** have usually bought the property and if they live in the property are often called **owner-occupiers**. There are many different kinds of **tenancies** each according the **tenant** different rights, eg **secure tenancies, assured tenancies, assured shorthold tenancies** and **protected tenancies**.
tenure diversification	Changing the **tenure** composition of a particular area away from one single **tenure**, eg from just council housing to include **owner-occupiers** and private renters.
THERMIE	A European programme supporting projects to develop new technologies for **energy efficiency** in building and the use of solar, wind and other forms of renewable energy.
Third Reading	Final stage of a **Bill's** passage through Parliament. It follows **Report Stage** and allows the full House to take an overview of the amended **Bill**. Substantive amendments are not usually possible at this stage.
threatened with homelessness	Statutory definition applied to an applicant for housing who is likely to become **homeless** within the next 28 days. Applicants who are threatened with homelessness are assessed for re-housing in the same way as applicants who are currently **homeless**.
tolerance	The transfer of expenditure or funds from one year to another.
top-slicing	Earmarking resources for a specific purpose, often used by **central government** to finance new initiatives.
tort	A civil wrong entitling the person wronged to claim compensation (damages) or to take court action for an **injunction** to prevent a repetition. Examples of torts include **trespass**, assault, interference with goods and **nuisance**. Some torts are also criminal offences, eg assault.
Total Cost Indicators	A system of suggested maximum costs for the provision of **housing association** dwellings, used by the **Housing Corporation**. TCIs vary both in relation to the size of the dwelling and the region of the country in which it is to be constructed. The figures are used to measure the relative efficiency of different schemes.

Total Quality Management	A management ethos which places emphasis on the delivery of quality services, rather than solving problems after they have occurred. **TQM** is seen by many as good practice in the delivery of housing services.
Totally Integrated Energy Solution	**Department of the Environment** marketing theme for use by the **energy efficiency** industry. It promotes an integrated approach based on 5 elements: • an efficient heating system • whole house insulation • controllable ventilation • attention to lighting energy use • advice to **tenants**.
Town & Country Planning Act 1990	Set out the framework for **planning obligations (Section 106 agreements)** as well as **structure plans, local plans, unitary development plans** and planning permission for new **developments**.
town council	See **local council**.
trading accounts	Income and expenditure statements for a service, based on charges levied for jobs done and the costs incurred.
Training and Enterprise Council	Private companies set up with government funding to support businesses and service organisations with grants and advice towards meeting training needs in their local area.
transfer	Term with two major meanings in housing. 1) a **tenant's** move from one property to another. 2) a document used to transfer the ownership of **freehold** or **leasehold** of land or buildings where the land or building has **registered title** or will be registered immediately after the transaction.
transfer association	A **housing association** set up through a **stock transfer** from a **local authority**.
transfer of engagements	Transfer of stock from an **Industrial and Provident Society housing association** to another **housing association** which has undertaken to fulfil its responsibilities. If either is a **registered housing association**, permission will be required from the **Housing Corporation**.
Transferable Discount Scheme	Welsh equivalent of the **Cash Incentive Scheme**.
Transitional Special Needs Management Allowance	Temporary scheme in England to cover the transition from **Hostel Deficit Grant** to **Special Needs Management Allowance**.
Treasury	**Central government** department responsible for public spending, monetary and fiscal policy, government bonds (**gilts**) and domestic demand management. The departmental head is the Chancellor of the Exchequer.
trespass	A **tort** committed by a person who illegally enters or occupies property. Where there is illegal entry, the person entitled to occupy

may take court action claiming compensation (damages) and requesting an **injunction** to restrain any further trespass. Where there is illegal occupation (eg by **squatters**) the person entitled to occupy may take court action for **repossession**. Most trespassing is not a criminal offence but it may become an offence to remain in certain circumstances if the trespasser has been asked to leave or ordered to leave by a court.

trickle transfer

Gradual **stock transfer**. Normally occurs as properties become empty.

trust

An arrangement where named individuals (the trustees) own and/or manage money or property for the benefit of other people (the beneficiaries). One example is a charity including a **charitable housing association**. In a **charitable housing association** the committee are trustees and the **tenants** and potential **tenants** are beneficiaries. A trust may be set up using a constitution, a set of rules or a **trust deed**.

trust deed

A means of setting up a **trust** where the object of the trust and how it is to be run are set out in **deed**.

TUPE regulations

Transfer of Undertakings (Protection of Employment) Regulations 1981 intended to protect the position of employees when services are transferred to another body.

UDC	**Urban Development Corporation**
UDP	**unitary development plan**
UNCHS	United Nations Centre for Human Settlements. Body responsible for **Habitat II**.
URA	**Urban Regeneration Agency**
UK Sustainable Development Strategy	UK government programme for achieving its **Agenda 21** commitment.
ultra vires	A decision or act taken by an officer or organisation which is beyond the powers conferred upon it in statute.
Under Secretary of State	See **junior minister**.
under-occupation	Refers to the level of under used properties and the proportion of homes which have un-used bedroom space.
Unemployment Benefit	A **non-means tested contributory**, **social security benefit** for claimants seeking work. Abolished in October 1996 and replaced by the **Job Seeker's Allowance**.
unfit dwelling	A dwelling which fails the **fitness standard**, ie it is categorised as **Unfit for Human Habitation** (or is **Below the Tolerable Standard**).
Unfit for Human Habitation	Statutory stock condition standard used in England, Wales & Northern Ireland and defined in the **Housing Act 1985**. Dwellings which are Unfit for Human Habitation qualify for extra levels of public support. The factors considered are repair, food preparation facilities, bath/shower, dampness, toilet, ventilation, heating, stability, drainage, lighting, water supply. In Scotland, the term **Below the Tolerable Standard** is used. The **English**, **Welsh and Northern Ireland House Condition Surveys** contain data about the level and distribution of unfitness.
Unified Investment Fund	Money available through **English Partnerships** for **environmental improvements**, job creation and inward investment promotion.
unintentionally homeless	A short hand phrase meaning *not intentionally homeless*. An individual is **intentionally homeless** if s/he deliberately does or fails to do anything which results in them ceasing to occupy accommodation and which it was **reasonable** for them to continue to occupy. The **local authority** only has a statutory duty to provide housing to households if they are: • **homeless** or **threatened with homelessness** • **eligible for assistance** • in **priority need** • unintentionally homeless • and there is no other suitable accommodation in the area. If an applicant is **homeless** (or **threatened with homelessness**), **eligible for assistance**, in **priority need** but **intentionally homeless** the **local authority's** only duty is to ensure that accommodation is available on a short-term basis so as to give the applicant a **reasonable** opportunity to find their own accommodation.

unit	A property in which one household could be expected to live, from a one person flat to a five bedroom house. A **landlord's** stock is usually measured in terms of units.
unitary authority	A council which has responsibility for all the **local government** functions in its area, unlike two-tier authorities which divide responsibilities between **county councils** and **district councils**. All **metropolitan authorities** are unitary and all councils in Wales and Scotland are unitary following the **Local Government Review**.
unitary development plan	**Development plan** for **metropolitan authorities**. Comprises a **structure plan** (part 1) and a **local plan** (part 2) in one.
unreasonable	See **reasonable**.
unregistered title	The title to a property which is not registered at **HM Land Registry** in England or Wales. To prove ownership, the owner must produce the old **deeds** which show how the ownership has been **transferred** to them since a sale or **mortgage** that took place at least 15 years before.
Urban Development Corporation	Government funded agencies in England & Wales set up to regenerate run down inner-city areas. **UDCs** aim to bring land and buildings into effective use, encourage the development of industry and commerce and ensure housing and social facilities are available to encourage people to live and work in its area. **UDCs** are vested with the planning powers of a **local authority** as well as having the capacity to purchase land and resell it for profit. Eleven **UDCs** were started in the early 1980s and are now all being wound-down, their funding is being diverted into the **Single Regeneration Budget**.
Urban Pilot Projects	A European Union programme which the **European Commission** considers innovative and worthy of receiving **ERDF** money (even in areas which fall outside of the funds objectives). To be eligible, projects should: • address a theme of urban planning or regeneration of European interest • be innovative and offer new approaches • produce lessons which are applicable to other cities • contribute to the development of the region where the city is situated. Many housing projects have been successful in attracting Urban Pilot Projects funding.
Urban Programme	**DoE** scheme designed to tackle economic, environmental and social problems in inner city areas. Funds were made available to **local authorities** seeking to support industry in the form of loans or grants. The money was principally for **environmental improvements**, renovating industrial buildings, site preparation, rental on newly leased business premises and establishing co-operative enterprises. The Urban Programme has subsequently been folded and its funding directed into the **Single Regeneration Budget**.
Urban Regeneration Agency	See **English Partnerships**.

usable receipt

The proportion of **capital receipts** which a **local authority** can spend, currently set at 25% for housing receipts. The usable proportion of **capital receipts** generated from non-housing sources is 50%. The non-usable (or **reserved**) proportion must go towards off-setting any debts the **authority** may have.

U-values

Rate at which buildings lose heat, measured in Watts/Square Metre/°C. 1990 building regulations recommend U-values of:
- Walls   0.45
- Roofs   0.25
- Floors   0.45.

VAT	Value Added Tax
VBM	**voluntary board member**
VCT	**voluntary competitive tendering**
VFM	Value For Money
VPG	**Voluntary Purchase Grant**
Value Added Tax	Sales tax payable on a wide range of goods and services. The current rate of **VAT** is 17.5% except for the 8% levied on gas and electricity. Only organisations with a turnover exceeding £40,000 need to pay this tax.
value analysis	Method of calculating the value of service relative to the cost.
violent profits	See **mesne profits**.
virement	The transfer of expenditure from one use or project to another or from one budget to another.
void	An empty dwelling.
voluntary board member	Unpaid member of the **board** of a **housing association**.
voluntary competitive tendering	Voluntary **tendering** process which some organisations go through to **contract** out certain functions and services, usually in advance of **CCT**.
Voluntary Purchase Grant	New scheme launched in the **Housing Act 1996**, encouraging **housing association tenants** to purchase their homes at a discounted rate in much the same way as **right to buy** operates. Participating **housing associations** will have to offer all their **tenants** the opportunity, except for those in homes built with **Section 106 agreements** and those in rural areas of fewer than 3,000 dwellings.
voluntary transfer	See **Large Scale Voluntary Transfer**.

WFHA	Welsh Federation of Housing Associations
WHATS	Welsh Housing Associations' Tenancies & Sales database
WHCS	Welsh House Condition Survey
waiting list	**Housing register** of people seeking to be re-housed by a **local authority** or **housing association**.
warden	Locally based officer providing support and care services to **sheltered** and **supported housing** projects. The warden's role includes general support, handling emergencies and building management. Often seen as performing a good neighbour role.
Welsh Development Agency	Government body with responsibility for regenerating the Welsh economy and improving the environment. Its activities include urban and rural development programmes, property development, land reclamation and **environmental improvements**.
Welsh Federation of Housing Associations	Organisation which represents the views of **housing association**s in Wales. Welsh counterpart of **Scottish** and **National Federations of Housing Associations**.
Welsh House Condition Survey	Welsh counterpart of the **English House Condition Survey**.
Welsh Housing Associations' Tenancies & Sales database	Welsh version of **CORE**, funded by **Tai Cymru**.
Welsh Local Government Association	The part of the **Local Government Association** with responsibility for Wales. It is the successor body to the **Council of Welsh Districts** and the Assembly of Welsh Counties.
Welsh Office	**Central government** department which oversees Welsh affairs, headed by the **Secretary of State** for Wales.
Welsh Tenants' Federation	Organisation which represents the views of **tenants' associations** throughout Wales.
wheelchair housing	Housing designed or adapted specifically for use by wheelchair dependent residents, it provides more special features than **mobility housing**, including:

- access to the house from a covered carport or garage
- waist height door handles, window latches and switches
- knee spaces under cooker hobs, sinks and work surfaces
- a lift to the first floor
- sufficient space to manoeuvre a wheelchair
- baths with rails and wheelchair access platforms
- ceilings capable of holding hoists
- located close to local amenities.

Mobility housing tends to be tailor-made with a particular occupant in mind including possible future needs they may have.

White Paper	Document outlining the government's views on an issue of concern and setting down an agenda leading towards legislation, eg *Our Future Homes*. May be preceded by a **Green Paper**.

Widdecombe Report	A landmark report which outlined the restrictions on **local government** officers with particular respect to political activities.
women's refuge	Housing project providing safe and secure accommodation to women fleeing domestic violence.
working capital	The excess of current **assets** over current **liabilities** in an organisation's accounts. Used as an indicator of **liquidity**.
write offs	Debts which the creditor has ceased to recover and has no expectation of recovering, the most common of which are **former tenants' arrears**. Also known as **bad debts**.

yield

The income from an investment, usually expressed as a percentage of its cost price.

zoning

Reservation of specific areas of land for specific uses.

Z-scores

A measure of social and economic deprivation used by the **DoE**. The scores are based on house condition statistics, unemployment figures, numbers of single parent families, prevalence of ethnic minority etc.